Good Morning, Everybody!

BOOK 2

A Primary School Assembly Book

REDVERS BRANDLING

Published in 2002 by:
Nelson Thornes Ltd
Delta Place
27 Bath Road
CHELTENHAM
GL53 7TH
United Kingdom

02 03 04 05 06 / 10 9 8 7 6 5 4 3 2 1

A catalogue record for this book is available from the British Library

ISBN 0 7487 5872 0

Page make-up by Florence Production Ltd, Stoodleigh, Devon

Printed and bound in Spain by GraphyCems

Contents

Class assemblies

Drama in assembly

Assembly scripts

Story scripts

Scripted plays

Resources

Acknowledgements

I am, as always, grateful to the staff and children of the various schools I have worked in.

From them I learnt so much by watching and listening to a great many assembly presentations.

I am indebted to books mentioned in the text of this work. They have been sources of both inspiration and information. Some of the stories in this book have been used, heard and readapted several times in assemblies. Thus their original sources are not remembered and if this has unwittingly caused the infringement of copyright, the author apologises and will correct this omission in future editions if notified.

Finally I would like to thank the many people who found *Good Morning Everybody* useful, thus creating the apparent need for *Good Morning Everybody Book 2*.

My thanks are also due to Mary Maggs of Nelson Thornes for making the latter possible.

Introduction

Following a review of the National Curriculum some interesting comments regarding our aims for children were expressed such as: 'to equip them with values, skills and knowledge to deal with difficult moral and social questions; to be aware that people and other living things have needs and that pupils have some responsibilities in meeting them; to identify and show respect for differences and similarities between people; and to recognise that family and friends care for each other' (SCAA, 1999).

If we set these comments against the idea that 'religious education starts with where people are, and as they are' from G. Bennett and I. Tiernan (illus.), *Hello World* (1972), the combination illustrates why the primary school assembly should be such a challenging, stimulating, demanding, and yet ultimately rewarding occasion.

Young children have very limited experience and yet at a practical level they have already encountered issues such as concern, sharing, joy, compassion and forgiveness, etc. Good assemblies build on this experience, extending it and providing opportunities for increased involvement.

This book is designed to help in meeting these aims. There are three main sections:

SECTION 1

This provides direct assembly material in the shape of seventy complete assemblies. Each of these has an introduction, a story, a prayer, hymn suggestion and additional information for the teacher. All of these assemblies could be used instantly with little or no preparation. However, their quality would be enhanced considerably with a little preparation and a personal approach. The stories chosen come from a wide variety of sources including folk tales, religious books, magazines, poems and factual accounts. They are divided into four main themes: People, Qualities, Creatures and Special Occasions. There are many other interwoven topics within these broad themes which teachers can draw out as and when they choose.

SECTION 2

This offers ten detailed assemblies which involve children in class presentations. These obviously require teacher/children/classroom preparation but will provide considerable opportunities for celebrating together. The section on class assemblies provides initial background information on the purpose or aim of each assembly and describes materials needed, necessary preparation and numbers involved.

Teachers will require little reminding that class assemblies should not be too frequent. As a rough guide, one class assembly per class per term is ideal. This allows plenty of time for preparation and also gives the children the sense of being involved in something special. Inviting parents will enhance the occasion.

SECTION 3

This concentrates on the use of drama in assembly. It is focused on the following areas: drama where there is action, linked with reading from scripts; drama where there is miming to a commentary; and drama where the action has been scripted, cast, learnt and presented in play form.

This section also provides starter ideas from a wide variety of sources. These can be developed by teachers as they choose. Some of these are looked at in more detail and expanded into scripted plays.

The overall aim of the book is essentially practical. It provides a range of material which can be used instantly; which can be developed along individual lines; and which can be as wide ranging as the teacher chooses to make it. The material chosen is intended to fulfil the needs of a multicultural environment. Finally, the presentation is as clear as possible, in order that the busy teacher is not faced with complicated cross-referencing in the search for lively and thought-provoking assemblies.

Hymns used are from *The Complete Come and Praise* (BBC Educational Books, 2000) and biblical quotations are from The Good News Bible. Dates of religious festivals, where given, are approximate.

Complete assemblies

PEOPLE

1 JAMIE'S BOOTS

INTRODUCTION

Do you own something that is a special treasure to you? It might be a doll, or a favourite book, a hat or a model. This morning's story is about a boy who treasured above all else his . . . well, listen and you'll find out.

STORY

Jamie loved his football boots. They were dark red with white laces and made of very soft leather. He cleaned them every day and slept with them under his bed. They had been a present from his grandad.

However, although Jamie had the best football boots in Appleby Street School he was very far from being the school's best footballer. In fact, he wasn't much good at all.

He tried really hard and he never gave up but his passes always went to the other team, his shots were never on target and he was a slow runner.

Mr Hodgson, the teacher who taught the football team, sometimes let Jamie be a substitute but he rarely got to play. When he was a sub, Jamie would be there ready on the touch-line with his gleaming boots tightly laced and shining – all prepared if Mr Hodgson called him.

The star of Appleby Street was Lee Logan, who was everything Jamie wasn't. Fast and fierce, he scored goals nearly every game, even though his boots were dirty, old and were falling to bits. Lee didn't like Jamie and was always poking fun at him.

It was a cold rainy afternoon when Appleby Street played their most important game of the season. This was a very important cup match and there were lots of parents, teachers and children round the field as the teams ran out. Jamie was on the touch-line as usual but only ten of the Appleby Street team were on the field. Mr Hodgson was talking on the line to the eleventh member of the side.

'I'm fed up with you forgetting your boots, Lee, so you're not playing. Jamie will take your place.'

'But . . .'

'No buts.'

Jamie heard this. He felt a sudden thrill – he was going to play! Then, another thought burst into his head. This match was very important for the school. Lee Logan was a much better player than he was and Jamie knew Lee took the same size boots as him. Before he could stop himself, Jamie trotted up to Mr Hodgson.

'Sir, Lee can borrow my boots. He takes the same size.'

At first Mr Hodgson didn't say anything. Lee Logan's mouth gaped open in amazement and they both looked down at the sparkling red boots.

A minute later Jamie's precious boots, which had never been on anybody else's feet, were ploughing through the mud on the bottom of Lee Logan's sturdy legs. And he made good use of them! Appleby Street won and Lee scored both goals.

Well, I'm sorry to have to say that Jamie never did become a good footballer but he certainly became one of the most popular children in the school. And his special friend would never let anybody say anything against him. I don't need to tell you what his name was, do I?

PRAYER

Let us think this morning about how it is sometimes very difficult to lend or give something we really value to someone else. It is especially difficult when that person is not a friend, or perhaps doesn't even like us. Let us pray that we might always be as kind as we possibly can.

HYMN

'You shall go out with joy' No 98 *The Complete Come and Praise*

Information for the teacher

1. The theme of this assembly could be developed further to take in more serious examples of thought and consideration for others, even to issues of self-sacrifice in certain contexts (for example, St Alban).

2. There are several quotations which might be useful here:
   'Be worthy of a reputation' (Confucius).
   'He is best loved who does most good to others' (Islam).
   'If your brother sins, rebuke him, and if he repents, forgive him. If he sins against you seven times in one day, and each time he comes to you saying, "I repent," you must forgive him.' (Luke 17:3–4).

---

2 FOR YOUR OWN GOOD

INTRODUCTION
'Darren, it's time to go to bed.'
'Do I have to?'
'Yes, it's for your own good.'
We can hear something like this every night in homes all over the world. Older, sensible people telling us to do something for our own good. Sometimes, however, children don't listen. This morning's story tells us of what happened to someone who didn't.

STORY
Have you ever wondered why there is only one sun in the sky? Well, the Chinese have a story which explains this.

The god of the eastern sky was Di Jun and he had ten sons. Each morning one of the sons was taken in his mother's chariot high into the sky. Then he had to walk across the sky to give light and warmth. You see each 'son' was a 'sun'.

After hundreds of years of doing this, the sons became bored.

'Same old stuff every day,' moaned Son Number 1.

'It's so boring,' continued Son Number 2.

'Ah, but I've got an idea,' interrupted Son Number 9.

'Come on. Tell us,' urged Son Number 10.

'Why don't we all go into the sky together one morning?'

'Fantastic!'

'What a brilliant idea!'

One morning, before their mother awoke, the sons crept out and began to walk across the sky together. As the morning wore on you can imagine what began to happen. Instead of one sun, there were ten. The earth became hotter and hotter. Rivers began to dry up, plants shrivelled, animals gasped and people fainted – it was a disaster.

Emperor Shun sent for Di Jun.

'This is terrible,' he protested. 'Get your sons back to doing their jobs properly at once!'

So Di Jun called to his sons once, twice and a third time. But they took no notice at all and things became hotter and hotter. Finally, and very sadly, Di Jun realised that his sons were not going to do as they were told and that the world would die if they were not stopped. He sent for the god of archers.

'Yes, what do you want of me?' asked the archer, leaning on his great bow.

Di Jun explained. Then the archer put a magic arrow into his bow and fired. The arrow streaked through the sky and hit a sun. It exploded instantly and turned into a bird.

Arrow after arrow hurtled through the sky and sun after sun was shot down. With one arrow left the archer took aim again.

'No!' shouted Di Jun.

He realised that if the last sun was shot down the earth could never have heat or light again. Hearing the shout, the archer put down his bow. And that is why we now have only one sun in the sky.

PRAYER
Let us pray this morning that we have the sense to listen to those people who give us advice for our own good. Let us give thanks that there are so many wise and helpful people in the world.

HYMN
'Think of a world without any flowers' No 17 *The Complete Come and Praise*

Information for the teacher
1. A very useful book for assembly material is Sandy Shepherd's *Myths and Legends from Around the World* (Evans Brothers, 1996).

2. In a Chinese context, the sayings of Confucius provide many thought-provoking ideas for assemblies. For instance, the following saying is linked loosely to the introduction to this story: 'The poor man finds it hard not to complain, the rich man finds it hard not to boast.'

---

3 MARGERETA

INTRODUCTION
We all like doing things which are exciting. Sometimes you need courage to do exciting things, such as diving into a swimming pool for the first time, or your first bike ride. This morning's story is about a woman who did something exciting and daring. There was something unusual about her though. You will find out what that was when you listen to her story.

STORY
'Are you okay?', the pilot's voice called out above the roar of the aeroplane's engines.

'I'm fine. How long to go?'

As she spoke, Margereta McMahon tugged at the straps of her parachute harness. Everything seemed tight and secure which stopped her feeling so nervous.

'We're still climbing,' answered the pilot. 'We have to reach over 3,000 metres. We should be there in about five minutes.'

Margereta looked out of the window. Far below her, the patchwork of fields shone in the morning sunshine. A thin spiral of smoke twisted up from a distant chimney and a train arrowed silently through the peaceful countryside. As she looked out, she heard a change in the sound of the engines. The noise from the plane straining to reach height as it climbed had stopped. The engines now sounded much more relaxed.

'Time to get ready, Margereta,' the pilot called. 'We are nearly at 4,000 metres now and we are right over the dropping zone. You'll get a countdown to your jump.'

Margereta pulled her straps even tighter. The aeroplane's door was now open and the wind was rushing past.

'10 . . . 9 . . . 8 . . . 7 . . .'

Margereta took a deep breath.

'6 . . . 5 . . . 4 . . . 3 . . .'

She shut her eyes.

'2 . . . 1.'

And then she was out of the plane. At first she was in a free fall without opening her parachute. She went faster and faster, falling at a tremendous speed.

Then – CRACK – above her the parachute opened. Soon she was swinging gently beneath the canopy enjoying the morning sun. Down below, the ground waited to welcome her.

'I enjoyed that!' shouted Margereta aloud.

But then she had lots of good memories. After all, she was 93 years old!

PRAYER

Let us think this morning about how much we can learn from people who have lived a long time. Let us give thanks in particular to grandfathers and grandmothers. We can be sure that nobody loves us more.

HYMN

'It's a new day' No 106 *The Complete Come and Praise*

Information for the teacher

1. There are plenty of opportunities to focus on the achievements of elderly people. One of the best sources here is the London Marathon. Beginning at Greenwich and ending at St James's Park, this 26 mile 300 yard race yields inspiring stories every year.

2. A useful address is The British Parachute Association (see p 195).

3. Margereta McMahon's jump took place in New Zealand in May 1999. Her descriptive comment was in keeping with her admirable spirit: 'It was like jumping off a kerb'.

---

4 HONESTY IS BEST

INTRODUCTION
Don't try to be too clever for your own good! This is good advice, as this morning's story will show.

STORY
There was once a king who had a beautiful daughter. One day she became very ill and the king ordered his best doctor to treat her.

'Your majesty,' said the doctor, after he had examined the princess, 'your daughter is very ill indeed but there is one thing which will cure her immediately. Somewhere in the kingdom there is a tree full of magic apples. If she eats one of these, she will be cured.'

The king stroked his chin anxiously. How was he to find the apple tree? He talked the matter over with his wisest minister.

'We must offer a reward,' said the minister. 'This is what we must do.'

So the king let it be known throughout his kingdom that anyone who brought the apple which would cure the princess would be given a title and many riches.

Now it so happened that there definitely was a magic apple tree in the kingdom and it belonged to a poor farmer who had three sons. He didn't know that the tree was magic but, like everyone else, he was keen to see if his apples could cure the princess.

'Right, John,' he said to his eldest son. 'Pick a basket of apples from our tree and take them to the palace for the princess.'

So John, who was a lazy and rude young man, set off with his basket of apples. On his way he met an old tramp.

'What have you got in your basket?' asked the tramp.

John looked at him scornfully.

'Pig's trotters,' he said sarcastically.

'Hmm,' muttered the tramp.

When John arrived at the palace, many others had been with apples before him.

'Here's another,' grumbled a tired servant. 'All right, give me your apples.'

Taking the basket from John he lifted the lid and saw pig's trotters!

John was immediately thrown out for insulting the princess.

When he got home his father was amazed to hear John's story.

'We'd better have another try,' he said.

So Alfred, the second son, set off with a basketful of apples. He hadn't travelled far before he met the old tramp.

Now Alfred thought he was very clever so, when the tramp asked him what was in the basket, he replied, 'Two fish, an old shoe and a pair of socks.'

Half an hour later, Alfred arrived at the palace. He found it even harder to get in but eventually he managed it. The same servant waited outside the princess's room to check the apples. When he lifted the cover he saw two fish, an old shoe and a pair of socks!

Alfred was thrown out of the palace so quickly that his feet didn't even touch the ground.

Well, the old farmer decided he'd have one last try with his youngest son. William wasn't like his brothers. He was very quiet, kind and hard-working. Soon he was on his way and, sure enough, the old tramp appeared.

'Good morning,' said William.

'It is indeed,' replied the tramp. 'What have you got in your basket?'

'Some apples which might cure the princess who is ill. But I'm sure I could spare one for you,' said William.

'Thank you,' answered the tramp.

When William arrived at the palace the servants were impressed by his good manners.

When they checked his basket they saw beautiful, rosy red apples.

Now it so happened that the king was passing by at the time.

'Mmm!' he exclaimed, 'I must say those are the very best apples I've seen. Wait here.'

So saying, he took the apples himself into the princess's room. Not ten minutes later he burst out of the room almost dancing with excitement.

'She's cured!' he cried. 'One bite was all it took. She's cured!'

There was cheering and clapping throughout the palace. The princess was better!

Now what became of William? Well, he was made a lord and became very rich. But he didn't change a bit. He was as kind and gentle as ever – something the princess found out for herself when she married him a short while later.

PRAYER

Let us treat everyone we meet as we would like them to treat us. Let us try to be kind and helpful without making a fuss about it.

HYMN

'Mother Teresa's prayer (Make us worthy, Lord)' No 94 *The Complete Come and Praise*

Information for the teacher

1. This story is very loosely adapted from one by the Brothers Grimm.

2. The apple carries great significance in Christian tradition. The Latin word *malum* means both 'apple' and 'evil'. The apple in the Garden of Eden was considered a forbidden fruit. In symbolic Christian art when the apple is shown with Adam and Eve it signifies sin. However, if shown in the hands of Christ it symbolises salvation.

---

5 DADS

INTRODUCTION

Dads are special people. This morning's story tells us about two boys who were very lucky to have their dad.

STORY

'Right lads, come on I'm going to take you fishing.'

Tony Jacques called out to his two sons as they were finishing breakfast.

'Okay, Dad.'

Lewis, who was nine, and Christopher, who was eight, were ready for any outdoor adventure. Half an hour later, complete with rods and bait the three of them were walking along a path beside the River Idle in Yorkshire.

'Now this is my favourite spot,' said Tony, as they reached a peaceful place on the river bank. 'Let's set up here.'

Once chairs, rods and gear had been set up the three settled down to fish.

But fishing is a sport that needs a great deal of patience and patience is something most children don't have a lot of.

'Dad,' posed Christopher, 'I'm bored.'

'What? We haven't been at it for an hour yet.'

'We haven't caught anything.'

'There's still plenty of time.'

Lewis joined in the conversation.

'Dad can we go and explore for a bit?'

Tony sighed.

'All right. But stay where I can see you.'

Suddenly the two boys were all energy. A few minutes later Lewis called out.

'Look at this fantastic sand hole we've found, Dad.'

Turning round Tony saw the two of them investigating a large pit of wet sand behind him.

'Keep away from that, it looks dangerous,' he warned, then turned his back because he thought he felt a fish take his bait.

Staring out over the river's surface Tony began to reel in his catch. Behind him he heard the laughing and shouting of his two sons. Suddenly there was a loud, wet thudding noise and then silence.

Tony turned urgently and was horrified at what he saw. Christopher had disappeared and all that remained of Lewis was his green wellies sticking out of the sand.

Dropping his fishing rod Tony dashed back to the sand hole. As he did so Christopher's head suddenly appeared out of the sand. He was screaming with fear. Only the movement of the wellies showed that Lewis was still alive.

Thrusting his large hands into the sand Tony began scooping it away from the thrashing wellies as fast as he could. Pouring with sweat he finally got as far as Lewis's waist and then, straining with all his might, he pulled the boy out. Now he turned to Christopher. Working with the same frenzy he got him free too.

Both boys were pale and gasping, and Tony realised that Lewis in particular couldn't breathe. Crashing back to their picnic bag Tony yanked out a large bottle of Coke and poured it in and over his sons' mouths, noses and ears to clear their airways. Gradually, spluttering and gasping, the two boys recovered.

Cuddling them tightly Tony spoke quietly.

'I think we'd better go home now, don't you?'

PRAYER

Dear God, Let us pray this morning for fathers all over the world. Help them in their task of bringing up their children and give them the resourcefulness needed to act in a crisis such as the one we have heard about this morning. Amen.

HYMN

'When your Father made the world' No 73 *The Complete Come and Praise*

Information for the teacher

1. This situation involving Tony Jacques and his two sons took place near Bawtry in South Yorkshire.

2. The way people react in emergency situations has yielded many inspiring stories which are suitable for use in assembly.

3. Warn children about the dangers of quicksand.

---

6 WHO WERE THEY?

INTRODUCTION

Nobody can win all the time in life. We all have our disappointments but how people deal with these tells us a lot about them. This morning's story is about how a very famous hero dealt with coming second in a contest.

But you will have to listen most carefully because throughout the story no names are going to be mentioned. At the end you have to guess who these famous people were.

STORY

Long ago a young man was walking through a forest. He was dressed in green, had a sword in his belt and a bow on his back. He whistled as he walked along and then he came to a bridge. The bridge was very narrow and there was another man standing on it. The man on the bridge was not just big and strong, he was huge!

Our hero stepped onto the bridge.

'I reckon he should get out of my way,' he thought.

The gigantic man had other ideas.

'I was here first. You wait until I cross,' he ordered.

Annoyed by this, our hero whipped his bow from his back and, as quick as lightning, fitted an arrow into it.

'Back,' he cried, 'or this arrow will help you on your way.'

The large man smiled contemptuously.

'So, you're a coward as well. Threaten a man with a bow and arrow when all he's got to defend himself is a simple staff.'

This angered our hero even further.

'I'll show you who's a coward,' he muttered angrily. 'You just wait until I get a staff too.'

Leaping from the bridge he quickly cut a thick branch from a nearby tree. His sharp knife rapidly sheared off the twigs.

'Now,' he cried, leaping back onto the bridge. 'Prepare to defend yourself.'

Within seconds the two men were hard at it. The sharp crack of their sticks echoed through the forest as they parried each other's blows. Then, with a sudden and mighty strike, his opponent caught our hero out and sent him hurtling into the river.

Gasping and spluttering he hauled himself out. Then he approached the stranger and held out his hand.

'Well done, my friend. You won that little joust fair and square. Now, my name is . . . and I'd very much like you to join my friends and me who live in this forest.'

Who were the two men?

PRAYER

Let us think this morning about accepting our disappointments and defeats graciously. Let us pray that we have the strength not to make excuses. Help us also to be modest in victory and success.

HYMN

'Guess how I feel?' No 89 *The Complete Come and Praise*

Information for the teacher

1. The two men were Robin Hood and Little John. Tales of the legendary Robin Hood offer an abundance of useful moral stories. For sources of further information, see p 195.

2. For a splendid, beautifully illustrated book on the outlaw's exploits, the following title is an excellent choice: Robert Leeson and Barbara Lofthouse (illus.), *The Story of Robin Hood* (Kingfisher, 1996).

---

7 WALLS

INTRODUCTION

Let us think for a moment about what walls do. They divide people from each other, they keep people out and they block things off. This morning, we're going to hear a Chinese story which is over two thousand years old.

STORY

Everybody called her Princess Blossom because she had such a beautiful garden. In the spring it looked and smelt wonderful with pink and white flowers. But Princess Blossom was far from her garden. The tears trickled down her cheeks as she peered through the dust. In front of her, thousands of men pulled and lifted great blocks of stone. The air was full of shouts and cries and gasps. Princess Blossom was watching the Great Wall of China being built.

'How can I find where he is buried?' she asked an overseer sadly.

'I can't help you,' replied the man roughly. 'The Emperor wants this wall built quickly. The work is hard and many people die every day. Your husband's body could be anywhere.'

Princess Blossom turned away. Her husband had been captured in a raid. As a prisoner he had been put to work on the wall. Then she had heard the terrible news. He had died trying to do the back-breaking work. Now all she wanted to do was to find his grave and take his body back to be buried in her lovely garden.

But, just as she stood beside a thorny bush, a strange voice called out to her.

'Princess, prick your finger on a thorn. Then hold it out in front of you and follow the drops of blood. They will lead you to your husband's grave.'

Princess Blossom looked round. There was no-one there. But she had heard the voice.

'Could it work?' she thought to herself.

Pricking her finger she held it out. Tiny drops of blood fell to the ground. She followed them. After just a few drops the blood suddenly dried up. She had found her husband's grave. Because she was a princess she was allowed to take the body back to her garden.

PRAYER

Let us pray this morning that we never build walls round ourselves. These sort of walls are built by being sullen, rude, unkind or selfish. Let us always welcome people – something walls never do.

HYMN

'Sad, puzzled eyes' No 74 *The Complete Come and Praise*

Information for the teacher

1. The Great Wall of China was built by the Emperor Shih huang-ti. It took ten years to complete, is about eight metres high and six thousand seven hundred kilometres long. To gauge the cruelty involved in its building it is said that for every stone in the wall a worker lost their life.

2. For a modern wall reference, Berlin is an obvious choice. Built in 1961, it was broken down in November 1989. In the years between it kept families and friends apart.

3. 'Barriers' is a common theme in RE. This material could be an addition to such a theme.

4. Perhaps as a direct opposite of the concept conjured up by walls, reference could be made to an old saying from Tibet: 'The greatest wealth consists of being charitable'.

8 DEAR GRAN AND GRANDAD

INTRODUCTION
This morning we are going to listen to a poem written by a nine-year-old girl to her grandparents.

POEM
Dear Gran and Grandad

Dear Gran and Grandad,
Do you remember when we went to *Cats*
And I spilt my ice cream
Down the lady in front?
Oh, it was awful!

Can you think of the time
When I sent you a letter
And the envelope came
With nothing inside?
Oh, it was awful!

And then what about
Last Christmas Day,
We all played 'Stations'
And I knocked down the tree.
Oh, it was awful!

But when I'm with you
And we talk of these things,
We have a good laugh and a joke,

That's when I'm
Terribly, terribly glad
That you're you and I'm me,
And that's . . . not awful!

Love, Jessica.

PRAYER

Our prayer this morning is also a poem.
Dear God,
This night when I'm asleep,
My family and friends
From harm please keep.
Amen.

HYMN

'I may speak' No 100 *The Complete Come and Praise*

Information for the teacher

1. Grandparents, particularly those who are retired, are often a valuable source of talent, remembrance and expertise for use in both classroom and assembly.

2. There is often a strong bond between children and older people. A useful quotation in this context might be: 'What has happened before will happen again. What has been done before will be done again. There is nothing new in the whole world' (Ecclesiastes 1:9).

---

9 ALL WRIGHT

INTRODUCTION

Every day we can look up into the sky and see an aeroplane flying overhead. Many of us go on holiday in planes. They also let families who are split up over various parts of the world visit each other. But how did it all begin?

STORY

'Well done, Orville.'

'How many's that?' said Orville back to his brother Wilbur as the two of them walked across the flat land of North Carolina in the USA.

Behind them their glider lay motionless on the ground. Minutes before it had been swooping in the clear sky with Orville at the controls.

'I reckon that's one thousand flights we've made in the glider.'

'And now we're ready to put that engine in.'

With their arms round each other's shoulders, the two brothers chatted as they walked. It was 1903 and they were determined to make the first aeroplane which would fly under its own power. For months they had been searching to find an engine to put into a glider. When they couldn't get what they wanted they decided to make an engine of their own. Now it was ready.

For the next few weeks they worked really hard putting the engine into a completely new plane they had built.

'Ready at last,' gasped Wilbur late one night as he wiped his hands on a greasy rag.

'About time,' answered Orville, 'but I'm sure it's going to fly.'

'Well nobody in history has ever made a plane that can fly under its own power with a person controlling it before so . . .'

'But we're ready to try!' exclaimed Orville excitedly. 'And we'll ask everybody in Kitty Hawk to come and watch.'

Kitty Hawk was where the brothers lived. Just outside the town on December 17th 1903, the two brothers stood beside their plane, 'The Flyer'. It was cold and windy and they looked round to study the crowds who had come to see this historic moment. They were disappointed; only five people had turned up!

'They're the lucky ones,' said Orville. 'Come on, let's go.'

So Orville lay on the lower wing of the plane and started up its twelve horsepower engine. Wilbur ran alongside to steady the wings and 'The Flyer' began to move along the launching track faster . . . and faster . . . and then . . . it was in the air!

For twelve seconds 'The Flyer' was airborne and then it sank back to earth. The five spectators cheered and clapped. The story of flying had begun.

PRAYER
Thank you Lord for giving people courage and skills that their achievements might make it a better world for all of us to live in. Let us give thanks for our safety and health. Let us also ask that new human inventions continue to improve life for everyone.

HYMN
'You've got to move' No 107 *The Complete Come and Praise*

Information for the teacher
1. For those who want to follow up the Wright brothers' story, there were more flights made on this momentous day. The fourth one lasted for 59 seconds and covered 260m.

2. The Wright brothers by no means secured instant acclaim and it was not until 1908 that the US Signal Corps asked them to build a plane for the army. After that, their fame spread and they toured the USA and Europe giving flying demonstrations.

3. Linking flight with the theme of 'caring', there are stories readily available almost every week of planes being used to airlift supplies to the needy or rescue ill and injured people. Helicopters obviously feature prominently in these stories.

4. A useful biblical quotation in this and many other contexts is: 'Make good use of every opportunity you have' (Ephesians 5:16).

5. There is also an appropriate quotation from 'Asolando' by Robert Browning which might be used here: 'One who never turned his back but marched breast forward, never doubted clouds would break'.

---

10 A HARD LIFE

INTRODUCTION

If you had lived in Britain hundreds of years ago, you would have found life very different, as you will hear now.

STORY

John was always hungry. He had three meals a day. For breakfast there was rough, coarse bread with a little bit of goat's milk to drink. In the middle of the day there was a tiny piece of cheese and . . . bread. For supper there was soup made of beans and mushrooms and . . . bread. And that stayed the same every day of the week.

'Right, John, up you get.'

Every day John dreaded his father's call. After that breakfast, John worked from dawn until dusk on the lord's land. He dug and ploughed, sowed and planted, weeded and dug again.

But then came the dreadful day when he was ill.

'Where does it hurt?' asked his mother.

'Right here,' groaned John, pointing to his aching stomach.

'Well, we'll have to see the wise woman then.'

Everybody in the village called Old Meg, the 'wise woman'. When anybody felt ill, they went to see her. She looked and listened and then mixed a few herbs together. No matter what they looked or tasted like you took them and got better – if you were lucky!

John was lucky. In a few days he was better and then he heard the good news.

'No work tomorrow lad,' said his father. ''Tis the day of the fair.'

And so the next day John went to the fair. The first thing he saw was a bear, chained to a thick post which had been driven into the ground. Around the bear was a pack of dogs. These were all leaping up and trying to bite the bear. As they did so it lashed out with its savage paws, killing the dogs if it caught one of them. All round stood men cheering and shouting.

John felt sick as he saw this terrible cruelty. Then he heard another noise.

'What's that, Dad?' he asked.

'Oh, it's the drummer. Look over there.'

John saw a drummer hitting a drum for all he was worth.

The drummer was outside a tent and John thought he could hear screams of pain coming from inside the tent. As he watched, the tent flaps opened and a man staggered out holding his face.

'What's happened to him, Dad?' asked John anxiously.

'He's had toothache and he's been in that tent to get his tooth pulled out. I reckon it must hurt a lot, because they just pull it out, you know.'

'But why was the drum playing?'

'Well, why do you think?'

Soon it was time to go back. It was a walk of six miles so John was pretty tired by the time he arrived home.

PRAYER

This morning's story tells us something of what a hard, cruel life it was in medieval times. And yet from such a harsh time comes this lovely prayer:

Where love is,
There riches be,
Keep us all,
From poverty.

HYMN

'Bread for the world' No 75 *The Complete Come and Praise*

Information for the teacher

1. For peasants in medieval times only the hardiest reached forty years of age and early death in childhood was prolific and expected. Disease via dirty water, rats, etc. was rampant and doctors were few and usually unavailable to the poor. Surgery, minus anaesthetics and antiseptics, was conducted by men who doubled as barbers.

2. The theme of something good coming from horrible times could be pursued in other ways, for example: acts of bravery in wartime; acts of kindness in difficult surroundings such as the Good Samaritan; and courage during illness.

---

11 SAVED!

INTRODUCTION

This morning's story is about how a young man found himself in an impossible situation. It seemed absolutely certain that he would die, but did he?

STORY

'Cleared for take-off.'

The crisp tones in his earphones told pilot Sid Gerow that he could get the plane airborne. He was at the controls of a Boston Bomber and was taking it on a test flight. When he heard the message he gave a thumbs up to his observer, Harry Griffiths, and opened the throttles.

Minutes later the bomber was climbing high above Wayzata airfield in Minnesota, USA.

'Looks cold out there, Harry,' called Gerow on the intercom.

'Twenty five below!' replied Griffiths.

Now the plane was flying at 2,500 metres in a temperature of $-25°C$.

'Stand by for testing,' called the pilot.

Griffiths strapped himself in tightly as Gerow dived and banked and climbed. After half an hour the pilot decided that everything about the engines and controls was working perfectly.

'Okay, Harry,' said Sid. 'It's your turn now. Go down into the nose and test the bombsight.'

The bombsight was right in the nose of the plane and to reach it Harry had to climb over a perspex panel. He was just getting into position when there was a disaster.

The entry hatch in the nose of the plane suddenly snapped open and tore off in the howling gale. Unable to stop himself Harry fell through it instantly, just managing to grab the bombsight as he did so. Immediately he was in a desperate position. He had no parachute on, he couldn't climb back into the plane, the wind was trying to batter him away from his grip on the bombsight, and the temperature was absolutely freezing.

Back at the controls, Sid was aghast.

'How can I save him? What can I do? It's got to be quick.'

These thoughts raced through his mind as he looked at the snow-covered landscape far below. Then, just to his right, he saw the frozen waters of Lake St Louis stretching into the distance. He made an instant decision.

'Hang on, Harry! Hang on,' he called aloud as he eased the plane downwards in a shallow dive.

Lower and lower the plane dropped, nearer and nearer to the frozen lake.

By now Harry Griffiths was almost unconscious in the bitter cold. His hands were numb and he knew he couldn't hang on much longer.

'You can't be thinking of landing, Sid,' he thought as the ground got nearer and nearer. 'You'll kill me if you do.'

Then, as the ice-bound lake suddenly appeared beneath him, he knew what Sid Gerow was trying to do.

The plane sank lower and lower, until it was just a few metres above the ice. At the same time the pilot cut the speed as much as he dared. One hundred and fifty kilometres an hour was as slow as he dared go.

Harry knew it was now or never. Closing his eyes tightly he let go. He dropped like a stone and fell so fast that, when he hit the ice, he began to slide along it at a breathtaking pace. For well over a kilometre he hurtled over the frozen surface of the lake and then, in a flurry of snow and ice, he gradually came to a stop.

'Thanks, Sid,' he said aloud. Then, standing up, he limped unsteadily to the shore.

PRAYER
Let us give thanks this morning for the skill, courage, quick thinking and daring which enables some people to save the lives of others. Let us think particularly at this time of pilots everywhere, especially those who fly rescue helicopters.

HYMN
'Rejoice in the Lord always' No 95 *The Complete Come and Praise*

Information for the teacher
1. This incident took place in December 1942. The bomber was being tested prior to being flown over the Atlantic for service in World War 2. Gerow was 28 and Griffiths 20 years old at the time. After his dramatic escape, Griffiths was rushed to hospital. The next eight days of his life were a complete blank to him, but he made a full recovery, having suffered only severe bruising and mild frostbite.

2. A useful quotation here might be: 'Wise people are rewarded with wealth, but fools are known by their foolishness' (Proverbs 14:24).

---

12 DO YOU LIKE FOOTBALL?

INTRODUCTION
Football is very popular! Many boys and girls enjoy playing it; thousands of spectators go to watch it in huge stadiums; and matches are often televised. This morning's story is about football, but it might not be quite what you expect.

STORY
'Come on, son. Time for work.'

Meer Mohammad Khan heard his father's voice through the thick clouds of sleep. It seemed as if he had just got to bed, but then he was always so tired!

Meer thought briefly about the charity school he went to. He learned to read and write there but mostly he enjoyed going so that he could rest. There wasn't much rest in his life.

'Come on son, hurry up.'

Once again he heard his father's voice. This time it was urgent.

Fifteen minutes later Meer and his father were hurrying through the drab streets of the dour industrial city of Sialkot. This was in Northern Pakistan and was where Meer and his family lived and worked.

Now, you might think 'what has all this to do with football?' and the answer is a great deal.

Sialkot is the home of the football. Nearly all the footballs which are kicked about all over the world are made in Sialkot. Considering how many people play and watch football you might think this is good for the people who live there.

Meer's family are desperately poor and he has to work for ten to twelve hours every day to earn money. But it is the wage he gets for his work which is equally dreadful. For every hour of hand stitching footballs Meer earns about three pence.

Now, at the time this story was being written (whilst Meer was earning his three pence an hour for stitching footballs), Ronaldo, one of the world's most famous players, was supposedly earning £1,490 an hour for kicking one!

Do you think this is fair?

PRAYER

Let us pray this morning for all those people, all over the world, for whom life is unfair. Let us pray particularly for children whose lives are so hard that they cannot enjoy the fun of being young. Let us pray that they may be given hope and that their lives improve. Amen.

HYMN

'Sad, puzzled eyes' No 74 *The Complete Come and Praise*

Information for the teacher

1. Sialkot produces over a million footballs every year which is eighty percent of the world's global market. Meer is an obvious victim of child labour but many of his peers are in an even worse situation because they have to handle dangerous machinery or are in contact with toxic chemicals.

2. In contrast with the sadness of this story, some biblical quotations may be referred to:
   'When a woman is about to give birth, she is sad because her hour of suffering has come; but when the baby is born, she forgets her suffering, because she is happy that a baby has been born into the world' (John 16:21).
   'Then [Jesus] took a child and made him stand in front of them. He put his arms round him and said to them, "Whoever welcomes in my name one of these children, welcomes me" ' (Mark 9:36–37).

---

13 DON'T BE GREEDY

INTRODUCTION

Nobody likes people who are greedy and cheat to get more than their fair share of things. This morning's story is about a greedy man who learned his lesson.

STORY

The three friends were drinking coffee together.

'We've got to teach Abdul a lesson.'

'Yes, he's the greediest man in town. He'll cheat anybody to get something extra for himself.'

'Perhaps if we play a trick on him it will bring him to his senses.'

'Let's try it.'

So the next day Ali, one of the three friends, called at the house of Abdul, the greediest man in town.

'Abdul my friend,' began Ali. 'I am having a family party tomorrow and I haven't got a pot big enough to do the cooking. Could you lend me one, please?'

'No. I haven't got any that are big enough.'

'But I've seen you using one. I'll take good care of it.'

Abdul scowled as he thought. As a rule he never loaned anything to anybody. But, perhaps, if he loaned Ali this pot, he could borrow some food from him later and 'forget' to pay it back.

'All right,' he mumbled reluctantly. 'You can borrow my pot.'

Two days later Ali returned with the pot and there was a smaller pot inside it.

'What's this?' asked Abdul.

'Well, amazing really,' replied Ali. 'Whilst your pot was in my house it gave birth to this smaller one. So it is only right that you should have it.'

Abdul thought, 'a pot giving birth to another pot? Who ever heard of such rubbish! Still, best not to say anything. After all he had got an extra pot for nothing!'

'I see,' he said out loud. 'Yes, quite right. The pot should be mine.'

Over the next few weeks, Ali borrowed a pot from Abdul three more times. On each occasion the pot 'gave birth' so Abdul got two pots back. He liked this arrangement very much indeed!

Then one day Ali turned up again.

'What's the matter?' asked Abdul.

'The biggest party ever this week,' replied Ali. 'I need to borrow five big pots to do the cooking in. I don't suppose you've got that many?'

'Oh yes I have. Wait I'll get them for you.'

Abdul hurried away, rubbing his hands as he did so.

'Five pots,' he thought. 'I'll lend him five and I'll get ten back. That's what I call good business.'

After two days, however, Ali had not brought the pots back. Two more days went by and then two more. Abdul was getting worried and angry.

'Where are my ten pots?' he thought to himself. 'I can't wait any longer. I'm going to get them.'

Abdul marched round to Ali's house and hammered on the door.

'My pots,' he snapped, when Ali appeared. 'My pots, you haven't . . .'

He stopped. Ali's head was bowed. Could he be . . . .was he crying?

'I'm so sorry,' whispered Ali.

'Sorry? What are you so sorry about?'

'Your pots . . . I can't return them.'

'What!' gasped a furious Abdul. 'You can't return them. What do you mean?

'They've died,' sighed Ali.

'Died! Died! How can a pot die?' shrieked Abdul.

Ali looked slyly from behind his hand.

'The same way as a pot can give birth,' he said quietly.

For a moment Abdul stood there and said nothing. Then, slowly and reluctantly, he smiled. He'd seen the trick and, what's more, he realised why it had been played on him.

'I think I've learned my lesson,' he said, equally quietly.

PRAYER

Let us think this morning about the words of a very old and famous prayer:

Let us give and not count the cost, work and not look for rest or always think about what is the reward (adapted from the prayer of St Ignatius).

HYMN

'A still small voice' No 96 *The Complete Come and Praise*

Information for the teacher

1. A little aside with regard to greed and cheating is that when Turkish bakers were discovered to have cheated their customers in bygone days they were nailed to the bakery doors by their ears!

2. A useful quotation concerning greed is: 'If you love money, you will never be satisfied; if you long to be rich, you will never get all you want' (Ecclesiastes 5:10).

---

14 TALES A DIARY TELLS US

INTRODUCTION
Sometimes we can learn an awful lot from a diary. If, for instance, some-body had been keeping a diary for the Royal National Lifeboat Institution, they might have made entries like the following for two dates in 1999.

STORY
24th April

Off the south coast of Britain a container vessel, the *Ever Decent*, col-lided with a cruise liner, the *Norwegian Dream*. Lifeboats from Dover, Margate and Ramsgate were alerted and raced to the scene of the collision. Although damaged, the *Norwegian Dream* did not need help and limped into Dover harbour.

It was very different aboard the *Ever Decent*. A serious fire had broken out aboard this ship and poisonous smoke was pouring from it. Bravely and skilfully the lifeboat crew approached the stern of the ship and took six men off it. The lifeboats then stood by for eighteen hours whilst the fire was fought and eventually brought under control. No lives were lost.

2nd September

The lifeboats at Hoylake and New Brighton received an SOS. A fishing boat called the *Progress* was on fire and the crew were desperately fighting the blaze. A man was badly injured during this attempt to put the fire out and lifeboats rushed to the rescue. Two lifeboatmen volunteered to board the stranded vessel. They then took off the injured man and he was rushed back to hospital at Hoylake. No lives were lost.

No matter how skilled people are at making ships, there are still acci-dents aboard them. Similarly, we never know when storms at sea are going to cause great danger to sailors.

The RNLI was founded in 1824 and since then there have been over 175,000 launches which have saved 134,000 lives. What stories of bravery a diary of all these rescues could tell.

PRAYER
Let us pray this morning for all those whose lives are spent helping others in dangerous conditions and situations. We think especially of those who work in rescue at sea and give thanks for all the lives they have saved.

HYMN
'Waves are beating' No 84 *The Complete Come and Praise*

Information for the teacher
1. The daily cost of the RNLI in 2000 was £240,000. For sources of further information, see p 196.

2. Courage at sea is a theme which can be developed via many routes, with stories from Grace Darling onwards. In winter months particularly, national newspapers are a valuable source here.

3. Developing the diary theme, the diary of Samuel Pepys is a useful source. There is plenty of scope for building up a class or school diary to show commendable things which have happened locally.

4. A useful, and salutary, quotation might be: 'Sailors tell about the dangers of the sea, and we listen to their tales in amazement' (Ecclesiasticus 43:24).

15 CHILD STARS

INTRODUCTION
This morning's story is about special children and you'll see why they are called this when you listen to their stories.

STORY
Let's start with Sarah Jones. Sarah was alone in the house with her mother one day, when suddenly her mother felt ill and fell to the floor. Now Sarah knew that her mum had been ill like this before from time to time. She also knew she had to do something about it and quickly!

She picked up the telephone and carefully dialled the emergency services number – '999'. Then she told the operator who she was and what had happened to her mum. She then gave her address and even remembered to say what medicine her mother had been taking.

Soon an ambulance arrived and Mrs Jones was given prompt treatment whilst a nurse took care of Sarah.

Nobody was more impressed by Sarah than Mrs Jones.

'We are all very proud of her,' she said. 'She probably saved my life.'

Then there's Adam Dennis, another primary school hero.

Adam and his friend Andrew Briggs were out playing in the snow.

'Race you down this slope,' challenged Andrew.

'You're on,' agreed Adam, as the two boys enjoyed themselves skidding and sliding about in the snow.

Then suddenly Andrew fell and didn't get up. Adam ran to help his friend and saw to his horror that he was unconscious. He didn't panic but thoughts raced through his head.

'I've got to do something. I can't move him and it might be dangerous if I do, but he needs help quickly.'

Fortunately there was a house nearby. Adam raced to it and told the owner exactly what had happened. As soon as he was given blankets, hot water and a hot drink, Adam rushed back to his friend. Meanwhile the houseowner called for an ambulance.

When Adam reached his friend, Andrew was coming round. Adam wrapped the injured boy in blankets then gave him a hot drink and the hot-water bottle, until the ambulance arrived.

Our last heroine was only six years old when she saved her four-year-old brother's life in a very different way. Paul was very ill with a disease which could only be treated by having a transplant from another healthy child.

'I'll help,' volunteered Debra.

So both she and Paul had operations and, thanks to Debra's courage, Paul made a marvellous recovery.

PRAYER

Dear God, Thank you for the inspiration we can get from other children. Thank you for the courage of so many young people and the gift of our eyes and ears so that we can know their stories. Amen.

HYMN

'From the tiny ant' No 79 *The Complete Come and Praise*

Information for the teacher

1. Paul, in the third story, was suffering from CGD (Chronic Granulomatous Disease), a defect of bone marrow genes. This is a hereditary disease which affects only about seventy families in Britain. The transplant from Debra was successful because she was not a carrier of CGD.

2. A useful quotation here might be: 'He is best loved who does most good to other creatures' (Islamic saying).

3. This assembly might be used as starting point to consider worthy acts by children in the school.

---

16 WHAT'S IN A NAME?

INTRODUCTION

This morning's story is a true one from Bangladesh. It might start you thinking about names.

STORY

It was hot, very hot. The river swirled back on either side of the motor launch as it ploughed steadily upstream.

'I've been looking forward to this journey for ages,' said Shoaib, mopping his brow with a large handkerchief.

'Oh,' replied Niten, 'why is that?'

'Well, I'm going home. I haven't been back for nearly a year. What's more I've saved a little money and I'm going to give my parents a treat with it.'

'Good for you,' continued Niten. 'I've been saving up too. It's taken me a long time but now I've got enough to buy my wife a really nice birthday present. I'm looking forward to seeing her face when she gets it!'

The two men chatted on. Around them were lots of other people, excited by this rare trip on the Ganges motor launch.

Meanwhile, at the controls, the captain opened up the throttles to get more speed.

'This is the bit,' he said worriedly to the sailor who was standing beside him. 'Keep a sharp look out.'

Both men gazed anxiously at the river bank. This was the loneliest stretch of the whole journey and it was here that a pirate boat made regular raids on launches which passed up and down the river.

'Maybe we'll be lucky this time,' said the sailor. 'At least they don't know about it,' he went on, nodding at the crowd of passengers as he spoke.

No sooner had he spoken than one of these passengers suddenly pointed a finger dead ahead. A fast boat was just swinging away from the shore.

'Captain, look!'

But the captain had already seen it. This wasn't going to be their lucky day after all.

Cramming on as much speed as he could, the captain tried desperately to escape from the pirates. It was no use. They had much more speed and within minutes they were alongside, with guns already out and pointing at the terrified passengers.

The villains clambered aboard pushing and shouting. They dragged out one passenger at a time and took everything valuable from them. Even the poorest were robbed of what little they had. Eventually the pirates were satisfied with their haul. Their leader pushed the captain of the launch roughly to the deck then scrambled back to his own ship. With a roar of motors and dense black clouds of smoke the pirate boat roared off down the river.

The poor robbed people gazed helplessly after it.

'One year's savings – all gone,' groaned Shoaib.

'My wife won't get that sari now,' muttered Niten.

'Criminals! Thieves! Villains! Robbers!' cried one old man after the departing pirate boat. Tears trickled down his face. He had lost everything.

PRAYER

Let us think this morning of some of the names we have heard in this story: thieves, robbers, villains, criminals and pirates. Let us think of the shame of being called by a name like this.

Let us pray that, by our actions we are called by a name we are proud of. Let us think of one in particular – friend.

HYMN
'Lead me from death to life' No 140 *The Complete Come and Praise*

Information for the teacher
1. This story stems from the activities of a group of pirates on the River Ganges, thirty miles south of Dacca in Bangladesh. They held up motor launches and robbed three thousand people. These victims were, in the main, very poor. The takings of the robbers amounted to £53,000.

2. This idea of names can be developed much more comprehensively, with stories which are appropriate. The negative side of names – fool, cheat, vandal, coward, liar, etc. – might be set against the more positive – helper, supporter, hero/heroine, saviour, carer, friend, etc.

---

17 WHAT A DAUGHTER!

INTRODUCTION
We are going to hear this morning about a very determined daughter. She felt angry that something most unfair had been done to her father and she was going to put it right!

STORY
'You will go to Siberia – now!'

When he heard the words Captain Jean Lopouloff was horrified. He was an officer at the Russian court and had happened to catch the emperor, Alexander the First, in a bad mood. Captain Lopouloff had irritated him and in a burst of temper the emperor spoke angrily.

However, once he had said something like this there was no going back and he never changed his mind. And so Captain Lopouloff, his wife and three-year-old daughter had to leave their comfortable St Petersburg house and were bundled off to the dreaded land of Siberia.

Siberia was two thousand miles away and a place of ice, snow and savage packs of roaming hungry wolves.

'I'm sure the emperor will pardon me,' said Jean to his family. 'After all I have done nothing wrong. I will write to him.'

The captain wrote letter after letter to the emperor. His friends in St Petersburg also sought a pardon for him. But nothing happened. The years went by in the bleak, miserable climate where the family was always cold and often hungry.

Eventually Prascovie, Captain Lopouloff's daughter, reached the age of fifteen. She looked at the poor, tired worn-out man who was her father one day and spoke with real determination.

'All those letters you wrote have done no good,' she said. 'I am going to see the emperor myself.'

'Ah Prascovie,' sighed her father. 'Travel two thousand miles by yourself – impossible! We haven't enough money to buy a sledge. How could you possibly make such a journey?'

Prascovie didn't answer and her parents thought she would forget about the whole idea. But she didn't and eventually she persuaded them to let her go.

'I'll give you all the money I have,' said her father.

So she set off. Her parents, however, were not worried.

'It's impossible, just like I said,' repeated the captain. 'She has enough money to get her started but she'll soon be back – you'll see.'

'I'm not so sure,' replied his wife, who knew just how brave and determined her daughter was.

So began Prascovie's nightmare journey. She walked for days through deep snow and spent her nights in poor village cottages. When her money ran out and she couldn't pay for lodgings she washed and worked for her night's stay. Some nights there was nowhere to stay and she slept in the woods, frozen and terrified of the prowling wolves. Once she spent the night on some church steps and was then given a lift on a passing sledge. This brought her to an inn. Now it was the depths of winter.

'You can't go on in this weather,' said the woman who owned the inn. 'You will die within a week.'

'But I have no money to pay for a long stay,' sighed Prascovie.

'You can work for me during the winter and then continue your journey in the spring,' said the woman.

And so Prascovie worked hard, washing, cleaning and doing any odd jobs which were required. But the kind woman helped her in return not only by letting her stay but also by teaching her how to read and write.

Finally spring arrived and Prascovie continued on her journey by boat. For a time this part of the trip went smoothly but then one dreadful day the boat hit a rock and sank with all its passengers still on board. Prascovie was one of the few who were rescued and she was taken to a nearby convent.

Once again she was very ill and the nuns had to look after her for many weeks. When she had recovered it was winter again and she had to stay even longer.

'We think you are a very brave girl,' said one of the nuns, when spring finally arrived again. 'So to help you, and your father, we have arranged for you to travel to St Petersburg by sledge.'

'Oh, thank you,' said the grateful Prascovie, now sure that she would get to her destination at last.

And so she reached St Petersburg, but there more disappointments awaited her. Try as she might she could not get to see the emperor, and no one would help her. It seemed that she was never going to succeed. One night she sat down and wrote a letter to the emperor. Then she went and stood in front of the huge statue of Peter the Great, Russia's most famous emperor.

'I'm going to climb up and put this letter in the statue's hand,' she thought. 'Someone might take notice of it.'

Then she started to climb the great statue. But she was so weak she kept falling back. Suddenly she heard a voice.

'What are you doing? My mistress wants to know what you are doing.'

Prascovie turned and saw a girl of her own age. Behind her was a magnificent coach with a rich lady sitting in it. Minutes later, Prascovie was telling the lady her story.

'Right,' said the lady when she had finished. 'You are coming home with me and then we'll see what we can do about this.'

And so, a few days later, Prascovie told her story to the emperor himself. When she had finished he nodded slowly.

'My dear, what you have done for your father is almost beyond belief. Therefore, he must be worthy of a pardon and I grant him one immediately.'

Can you imagine how Prascovie and her parents felt when they were soon back together again in St Petersburg?

PRAYER

Let us pray this morning for all kind and loving sons and daughters. Let us pray that we never let our parents down. Amen.

HYMN

'Give us hope, Lord' No 87 *The Complete Come and Praise*

Information for the teacher

The following biblical quotations could be linked to this mid-nineteenth century Russian story:

'Respect your father and your mother' (Exodus 20:12).

'Be prepared for times when you will be put to the test. Be sincere and determined. Keep calm when trouble comes' (Ecclesiasticus 2:1–2).

'There is more happiness in giving than in receiving' (Acts 20:35).

---

18 THANK YOU

INTRODUCTION

We all have disappointments in our lives and times when things don't work out as we hoped they would. This morning's story is about a man who was disappointed by his friends but that did not stop him helping others.

STORY

John was pleased with life. His business was doing well, he was happily married, he had a large comfortable house and he was very content.

'I want all my friends to share in my good fortune,' he thought to himself one day.

He then talked things over with his wife.

'Let's have a really good party,' he said. 'We'll get an expert cook in to make a fabulous meal and we'll have waiters to serve it. We'll decorate the house. Oh, it will be a lovely night.'

So John and his wife made the arrangements. For days wonderful food arrived at John's house; invitations to all his friends were sent out; and the cook and the waiters were booked for the great occasion.

Time went by until it was the day before the great feast. John and Marjorie, his wife, were looking at the replies to the invitations.

'Leroy and Merlene aren't coming – they're going on holiday.'

'Hmm, Walter's got an important business appointment and he can't make it.'

'Vijay and Jamila have to go and see Jamila's mother.'

'The Joneses are going to their son's for the weekend.'

'Just a minute, just a minute,' said John suddenly. 'If all these people can't come, who is coming?'

'Well . . .' began Marjorie, when the telephone interrupted her.

She came back with a rather long face.

'That was Bill and Jan. They're going to get a new dog so they can't come.'

'As I said,' snapped John impatiently, 'how many are coming?'

'Well, dear,' Marjorie replied hesitantly, 'I'm afraid . . . er . . . nobody.'

'Nobody! You mean we've arranged this fantastic meal and party and nobody – just nobody – wants to come?'

For a moment John's face was clouded with annoyance and disappointment. Then suddenly he gave an enormous smile.

'I know some people who will want to come,' he said quietly. 'Go ahead with the arrangements. We're going to make it the best party ever.'

The next day, shortly before the food was to be ready, John called the waiters together.

'Now,' he said to them, 'there are lots of homeless people on the streets. We're all going out to invite them back to my house to enjoy a great meal. Let's go.'

The homeless people of the town accepted his invitation. A wonderful meal and a happy night was enjoyed by all.

PRAYER

Let us try never to be ungrateful when people show us kindness. Let us try never to let disappointments make us miserable, bitter and bad-tempered. Let us always be willing to share with others. Amen.

HYMN

'I come like a beggar' No 90 *The Complete Come and Praise*

Information for the teacher

1. Teachers may recognise this adaptation of a well-known Bible story (Luke 14:17–24). It carried a warning from Jesus to the so-called religious people of the day that they should not ignore the invitation to listen to his message.

2. A story of a similar riposte concerns Guru Nanak. He was born in 1469 and spent his life advocating kindness and consideration to all. One day he was criticised by a Muslim for sleeping with his feet towards Mecca. His reply was: 'If you think it is wrong for me to point my feet towards the house of God, show me some direction in which God does not dwell'.

3. An appropriate quotation from Muhammad is: 'Visit the sick, feed the hungry, free the captives'.

19 PEOPLE OF THE YEAR

INTRODUCTION
There are many different ways of being brave. This morning we are going to hear about two of them.

STORY
Dan Holder is good at playing cricket. In fact, he is more than good, he is excellent. When he was a boy, he showed that he was one of the best cricketers in Gloucestershire. Because of this he was picked for the county under-sixteen team. He was a fast-bowler for this team but at first he found it very difficult to bat well for them. Then he got something which made it easier and he began to score lots of runs. In one game he scored a brilliant century of 131 not out.

Now you might say, 'what is brave about all that?' Well, Dan was born with only one arm. He achieved all this success playing against people with two arms. And the reason his batting improved was that he got a special artificial fitting which hooked onto the bat handle. Now he could really show them!

Another brave person is Carl Bougourd. Carl was a soldier who was training on a mountain in Alaska called Mount McKinley. Carl and the rest of the soldiers were at 6,500 metres when one of them was injured as they made their way down.

'Look,' said the injured man, Staff Sergeant Martin Spooner, 'you lot carry on down and get somebody to come back and rescue me.'

Now Carl knew this would never work. It would take days to get all this properly organised and even then it would be difficult to find Martin again. Apart from that he could do very little to help himself.

'No,' said Carl. 'The rest of you go on. I'm going to stay here with Martin until you can send help for him.'

And so the two men were left on the mountain. A freezing, bitter wind howled round them. Because they were on thick ice it was impossible to cut a hole to shelter in. All they could do was huddle as close as possible in their sleeping bags trying to keep each other warm.

'It won't be long. The others will soon get down and send somebody back for us.'

Carl tried to cheer up his injured companion.

Time passed very slowly . . . one day and night . . . another day and night. By the time a third day and night had gone by the two soldiers were very weak.

'We've got to keep talking,' gasped Martin.

'You're right, we've got to . . .'

Before Carl could continue a distant noise began to get louder and louder and then a helicopter burst into sight. They were saved!

Carl still had to pay a price for his courage in staying behind to look after Martin. His feet were badly injured with frost-bite.

'But anybody would have done what I did,' he said modestly.

PRAYER

Let us pray this morning that we might be brave when difficult things happen to us. Let us give thanks also for those brave people who risk their own lives to give help to others. Let us think especially of those whose work is to rescue people in trouble.

HYMN

'Guess how I feel?' No 89 *The Complete Come and Praise*

Information for the teacher

1. Dan and Carl were both chosen as 'People of the Year' in November 1999. This award ceremony is run by The Royal Association of Disability and Rehabilitation (RADAR) and has been an annual event since 1959. Similarly, the 'Children of Courage' awards ceremony takes place annually in December and receives wide media coverage. See p 195 for sources of further information.

2. A useful biblical quotation is: 'Be prepared for times when you will be put to the test. Be sincere and determined. Keep calm when trouble comes' (Ecclesiasticus 2:1–2).

---

20 TAKING ADVICE

INTRODUCTION

As we go through our lives we learn a tremendous amount from other people, if we are prepared to listen!

STORY

Jason wasn't like most new children.

When he came into the class he never stopped talking and it was all about himself.

'In my last house we had six bedrooms and you should have seen mine – it was absolutely huge. I bet it was the biggest bedroom a kid ever had.

My last teacher said I was great at football.

I can't wait until Sports Day because I'm a really good runner. I reckon I'll win lots of races.

The work in this school is dead easy.'

Jason was really a kind friendly boy. But, because he wouldn't stop talking about himself and boasting, none of the other children would have anything to do with him. He was always by himself in the playground, he was picked last for any team and nobody ever had a pencil they could lend him.

Miss Bywaters, the teacher, was concerned about this. One day she asked Jason to stay behind at playtime.

'Do you like poetry?' she asked.

'Yes Miss, I know a lot . . .' Jason began in his usual way.

'Well would you like to take this poem home with you tonight. Write it out in your work book and you can learn it off by heart if you like.'

This is the poem Jason wrote out:

The wise old owl sat high in an oak,

The more he heard the less he spoke,

The less he spoke the more he heard,

Why can't we all be like that wise old bird?

And do you know, Jason did learn that poem. And from that moment he stopped telling people how good he was and all he'd done and he became one of the most popular children in the class.

PRAYER

Dear Lord, Help us to learn from those we admire and respect. Teach us to listen and help us to gain the qualities of modesty, tolerance and common sense. Let us remember that we are never too old to learn.

HYMN

'I may speak' No 100 *The Complete Come and Praise*

Information for the teacher

1. There are plenty of fables which might be used in conjunction with this story, such as *The Boy Who Cried Wolf*.

2. A further discussion point here might be: 'It's not what we say, but what we do which counts'.

3. A relevant Bible story to illustrate boastfulness is the tale of the new barn (Luke 12:15–21).

21 THAT'S MINE!

INTRODUCTION
A prince called Siddhartha founded one of the world's great religions. He was called 'the Buddha' and many stories are told about him. Here is one of them.

STORY
One day the Buddha and a friend were walking by the river.

'Aren't they beautiful?' said the Buddha as he nodded towards some swans which were flying overhead.

'So graceful,' agreed Ananda, his friend.

But even as the two spoke there was a swishing noise and one of the swans staggered in its flight. A great arrow was sticking out from where its wing met its body and drops of blood fell into the river below.

'It's going to land near us!' cried Ananda.

Sure enough the wounded bird crashed down just in front of them.

'We must help it,' said the Buddha urgently.

He and Ananda raced up to the bird. Whilst Ananda held it, the Buddha knelt and, as gently as he could, eased the arrow out of its body. Then, tearing some strips from his clothes, he bandaged the wound, scraped a comfortable hole in the ground and laid the swan in it.

Whilst the two men were doing this, they heard the splashing sound of a boat being rowed from the other side of the river. Then, a furious man appeared beside them.

'That's my swan!' he shouted. 'I shot it with my arrow and I fired the arrow from my bow. So it's my swan.'

The Buddha looked calmly at him.

'I'm not surprised it was you who did it,' he sighed.

The man in front of him was Devadatta, his cousin. Now Devadatta was a jealous man who was constantly trying to cause trouble for the Buddha. He was always plotting against him.

'Did you hear?' he went on. 'That's my swan.'

'Hmm,' sighed the Buddha. 'Was it flying through your sky then? And was it your river it fell into?'

'It's . . .' Devadatta began again, but the Buddha wouldn't let him speak.

'Who do creatures belong to most? Those who try to kill them or those who care for them and seek to protect them?'

When Devadatta heard these words he had no answer. Grumbling and muttering he stormed off.

The Buddha and Ananda looked after the injured swan for a few weeks. When it was well again they took it back to the river where it joined the other swans.

PRAYER
Let us think this morning of all those people who care for sick, wounded and injured birds and animals. We give thanks for the work they do.

HYMN
'O let us spread the pollen of peace' No 145 *The Complete Come and Praise*

Information for the teacher
1. Siddhartha, the Buddha or Enlightened One, was born about 563 BC. A prophecy proclaimed that if he ever learned about sickness and death he would become a holy man instead of a king. His father, the king, wanted his son the prince to succeed him so he built a great palace to protect his son from the outside world. There, Siddhartha saw only riches and luxury until one day he went out and saw a dying man. After this he gave up his kingdom to do as much good as he could in the world.

2. Useful Buddhist references which might be used are:
   'Such is life, seven times down and seven times up' (Zen Buddhist saying).
   'When a person really cares about others he lights up the world, just as the moon does when it comes out from behind a cloud' (an adaptation of one of the Buddha's sayings).
   'The tree of wisdom has fibres of forbearance, deep roots of steadfastness, flowers of virtue, branches of awareness' (Buddhist saying).

---

22 WHAT IS IMPORTANT?

INTRODUCTION
Words are very precious things and often we use too many of them. This morning's story is about a man who knew how to use just the right number of words to say something very important.

STORY
Simon lived in the city of Babylon many years ago.

'I would like to become Jewish,' he said to a friend. 'But I would like to find out more about this faith first. I need to know what is really important about Jewish beliefs.'

'Ah,' said his friend. 'You'd better go and ask a rabbi. They are teachers of Jewish law. One of them will tell you all you want to know.'

'Hmm,' replied Simon, 'but teachers often talk too much. They use so many words that you lose track of what they are saying.'

'You could be right there,' continued the friend. 'Why don't you say you have only a short time to listen?'

'That's a very good idea,' agreed Simon, 'but I'll have to make absolutely sure they know I only have a very short time.'

'How will you do that?'

'Come with me and you'll find out.'

Simon and his friend went to see a rabbi called Shammai.

When they arrived, Simon spoke first.

'Could you help me, please?' he said.

'Certainly, certainly,' replied the busy-looking rabbi.

Then Simon did a funny thing. He lifted one foot up and stood wobbling on the other one.

'Can you tell me all I need to know about Judaism while I'm standing on one foot?'

This made Rabbi Shammai very angry.

'Don't waste my time with stupid games like this. Clear off the pair of you. Go on – get out!'

So Simon and his friend left.

Next they went to see a rabbi called Hillel.

Simon went through his routine again and there he was once more, hobbling about on one foot.

Rabbi Hillel gave a broad smile.

'Steady, steady,' he said. 'Yes, I'll be happy to help you. Just remember this – what is hateful to you, do not do to your neighbour.'

Simon put his foot down and went away feeling he had learned a very great truth.

PRAYER

Let us think about the message of this morning's story. Do we like to be laughed at, or bullied, or ignored, or made to feel unwelcome? Let us think about these things and pray that we always have the strength and sense to treat others as we would like them to treat us.

HYMN

'Simple gifts (Tis the gift to be simple)' No 97 *The Complete Come and Praise*

Information for the teacher

1. In the full version of this old Jewish story Rabbi Hillel supposedly said: 'What is hateful to you, do not do to your neighbour. That is the whole Torah [first five books of the Old Testament] and the rest is commentary; go and learn it'.

2. This story is a marvellous link to situations where there has been unacceptable behaviour from some children towards others in the school. The ideas of tolerance and intolerance could be explored more fully here.

3. One or two quotations might be useful:
'Be worthy of a reputation' (Confucius).
'Once a word has been allowed to escape it cannot be recalled' (Horace, the Roman poet who was born in 65 BC).
'You should each judge your own conduct. If it is good, then you can be proud of what you yourself have done, without having to compare it with what someone else has done' (Galatians 6:4).
'Just a single word that brings peace is better than a thousand useless words' (from the Dhammapada).

23 ST CECILIA

INTRODUCTION
Practically all of us like listening to some kind of music. There are many different types of music and they all please somebody. This morning's story is about somebody to whom music was very special.

STORY
Cecilia was asleep in bed. Then for some reason she felt restless and began to toss and turn.

'It must be morning,' she thought, 'as it is so light.'

Then she awoke fully.

'How strange,' she said to herself. 'It is light but I can hear music as well.'

The music did not sound as if it were being played on normal instruments. In an odd way, it was as if it was made up of the sounds of the countryside: birds, rivers and breezes blowing through trees. As Cecilia sat on her bed listening to the music and staring at the light she seemed to hear a message telling her that she ought to try to persuade more people to become Christians.

Then, as suddenly as they had come, the music and the light disappeared. Cecilia lay back on her bed.

'How strange and how marvellous,' she thought. 'Now I know what I have to do with my life.'

From the next day onwards, she spent the rest of her life telling people about Jesus. Now this was a dangerous thing to do because Cecilia lived in Rome, many years ago. At this time most people there were not Christians and those who said they were Christians were often killed or imprisoned. The Roman rulers considered them to be dangerous people.

This didn't stop Cecilia. But she kept thinking about the lovely music in her head.

'If I could tell people about Jesus and then play them some of the beautiful music, it might help them understand more easily.'

Cecilia set about learning to play every musical instrument she could find. But still she was not satisfied.

'None of them can make sounds like I heard on that wonderful night. There's only one thing to do. I'll have to invent a new instrument which does.'

As well as trying to teach people about Jesus, Cecilia set about inventing a new musical instrument. It is now thought that she might have invented the magnificent instrument we now know as the organ.

PRAYER

Let us give thanks this morning for music. Let us give thanks for all those musicians who entertain us with their skills. Let us give thanks for our voices with which we can sing. Let us give thanks for all those skilful people who invent and make musical instruments.

HYMN

'You shall go out with joy' No 98 *The Complete Come and Praise*

Information for the teacher

1. Very little is known about St Cecilia. It is thought that she was born into a non-Christian family and founded a church in the Trastevere part of Rome. She was recognised as a martyr in 545. She has been the patron saint of music since the sixteenth century and the organ is her emblem.

2. This is certainly an assembly which could be supplemented by spending more time than usual listening to some music. Personal choice and availability are always determining factors here but two relevant possibilities seem to be some organ music and some gospel singing.

3. There is a useful Shakespearean quotation which provides food for thought and discussion here. It would need to be adapted for use with young children:
'The man that hath no music in himself,
Nor is not mov'd with concord of sweet sounds,
Is fit for treasons, stratagems and spoils;
The motions of his spirit are dull as night,
And his affections dark as Erebus:
Let no such man be trusted' (*The Merchant of Venice* Act V Scene i Lines 93–98).

24 AREN'T WE LUCKY NOW?

INTRODUCTION

If we live in a big city in Britain today we expect to see attractive shops, buses, schools, churches, cinemas, sports grounds, warm houses and flats. We also expect not to be hungry, to go to the doctor's if we are ill and to go to school so that we can be educated. If we had lived in a city in Britain one hundred and fifty years ago, and been poor, life would have been very different.

STORY

'Hello, I'm Ben and I'm going to tell you a bit about my life. I live in London and the year is 1850.

My dad hasn't got much money and our family lives in two rooms. That wouldn't be so bad if there weren't so many of us. But there's four of us kids and the baby. Four in a bed keeps you warm but it's not very comfortable.

I'm dead lucky because I go to school. I don't like school all that much, but I only go in the mornings. I go to one of the schools they call "Ragged Schools" and the good thing about this is that they give you a pair of boots to wear. If I didn't have these I'd have to go about barefoot which is very cold in winter! I'll tell you something else too. Every day I have to walk half a mile with an empty pail to a drinking-water pipe. When I get there, I fill the pail right to the very top and then I carry it half a mile back home. Before I got my boots from school I had to do this trip in my bare feet and those stones and cobbles didn't half hurt.

At night all of us kids have to help Mum make matchboxes. Now you might think that is tricky but that's not the problem. It's hard because you have to work so fast! It is a really good job but we have to make over seventeen hundred matchboxes to earn ten pence.

I like Saturdays best of all because that's the day we have some bacon. The rest of the week we just have bread, potatoes, oatmeal and sometimes an onion. We have tea to drink though and I can remember once we had some mutton.

I reckon my mate Billy is really unlucky though. He's training to be a chimney-sweep. It's bad enough just thinking about crawling around those big dark filthy chimneys. The training's not much fun either. He told me his boss says you've got to get the skin hardened on your elbows and knees before you can start. You have to do this by rubbing brine on them in front of a hot fire. Billy says this hurts but if you don't do it the master sweep wallops you with his cane.

There's lots of kids around like me and Billy. Do you think you'd like to be one of us?'

PRAYER

Let us give thanks this morning for all those people who have worked hard to make a better life for children today. Let us give thanks for our food, our clothes, our homes, our safety and our schools. Let us pray too for those children all over the world for whom life is still very difficult.

HYMN
'In the bustle of the city' No 101 *The Complete Come and Praise*

Information for the teacher
1. The Ragged School Union provided many children with boots. An Act of Parliament in 1840 had prohibited young boys being trained as chimney-sweeps. Unfortunately, it was not adhered to and as late as the 1860s there were more little boys suffering in this job than ever.

2. There is plenty of scope for extending this theme to cover people such as Dr Barnardo and sources of further information can be found on p 194.

3. A useful quotation here might be: 'Help to carry one another's burdens' (Galatians 6:2).

---

25 ARTHUR POULTER VC

INTRODUCTION
The Victoria Cross is one of the highest military medals anyone can be awarded. In the stories of courage in war, the people who have won this award are very special indeed. Here is the story of one of them.

STORY
The date was 1918 and in France, British and German soldiers were fighting a terrible battle. The two armies were in trenches facing each other and from time to time each tried to cross the distance between these trenches. When they did so machine-gun fire killed and wounded hundreds of men.

Arthur Poulter, a 22-year-old British soldier, stood looking at the dreadful scene in front of him. He was a stretcher-bearer, which meant that, with another man, he had to carry wounded soldiers to safety on a stretcher.

'It's no good, Bill,' said Arthur to his partner. 'There's too many of them hurt out there. There's not time for two of us to go out and bring them back on a stretcher.'

'What do you mean?' asked Bill.

'It's quicker this way,' replied Arthur.

Then, without another word, Arthur climbed out of the trench, ran across the battlefield and began carrying wounded men to safety on his back. Shells and machine-gun bullets hurtled all round him as he did so. He paid no attention. His job was to save lives and that's what he was going to do!

Then the British soldiers heard an order ring out.

'Move back across the river!'

As the British troops retreated over the river, the Germans advanced towards them. Many of the British soldiers were hit as they tried to get away on the far side of the river.

'I've got to be more help here,' thought Arthur. He ran back quickly and picked up one of the men who had fallen.

'Right, now I must see to more of these lads,' he said to himself.

Even though the Germans were still firing, he set about bandaging the wounded men he had carried from the battlefield. Arthur managed to bandage and care for forty men skilfully and kindly.

Then, as he was returning for yet another one of the wounded, Arthur was hit and badly injured himself.

Finally the terrible war was over and, thankfully, Arthur recovered and went back home. But he was never forgotten. As one newspaper of the day said: 'This very gallant soldier's conduct throughout the whole day was a magnificent example to everybody'.

PRAYER

Let us give thanks for those very special people who risk their own lives to help and save others. Let us pray too for an end to all wars, wherever they may be. Amen.

HYMN

'The pilgrim's hymn (We ask that we live)' No 146 *The Complete Come and Praise*

Information for the teacher

1. Arthur Poulter's Victoria Cross was lost, and subsequently recovered in the years after 1918. In 1999 it was presented to his old regiment, Duke of Wellington's (West Riding Regiment), and now has a place of honour in the regimental museum in Halifax.

2. A comparable war story from a very different era concerns St Martin. He was a Roman soldier who lived c.316–400 and he decided that killing in wars of aggression was wrong. Therefore, he walked onto the battlefield carrying a cross. The most famous story of this saint, however, tells of when he met a naked beggar and immediately tore his soldier's cloak in half and gave one half to the beggar. That night he had a dream in which Christ came to him dressed in half a cloak and said: 'My friend Martin gave this to me'. St Martin is now the patron saint of France, soldiers and drapers.

---

26 THE STONES SAID 'NO'

INTRODUCTION

Look around at all the people in the hall. Some of the children might be older than you, some might be younger. Your teachers and helpers are all older than you. With this in mind, listen to this morning's story. It is an unusual one.

STORY

Long, long ago everything stayed the same in the world: the people, the animals, the birds and the stones. One day a rabbit was talking with his wife.

'Wouldn't it be lovely if there were some little rabbits instead of just us two?'

'Oh yes,' she replied. 'I would really like to look after some little rabbits. I can't think of anything better.'

'We could teach them to jump and burrow and . . .' continued the rabbit, until his wife interrupted him.

'Well, let's do something about it. We'll go and see the god who made the world and tell him what we think.'

So the two rabbits went to see the god who made the world and told him their thoughts.

There was a long pause as he looked carefully at them. Then he spoke.

'What you are talking about are children,' he said. 'Now you must think very carefully. I can give you children but, if I do, everything will change. They will grow and they will have children and their children will have children. Now if I let things go on like this the world will get far too full of rabbits. So rabbits will have to die to make room for the younger ones.'

The two rabbits looked at each other and smiled.

'We understand,' said the rabbit to the god who made the world, 'but we think that children would be so wonderful it would be worth it.'

So, the rabbits went back to their burrow and soon there were little rabbits everywhere!

They hopped and bobbed and jumped and rolled and it was a joy just to look at them.

'What fun they're having,' smiled Mrs Rabbit.

'They certainly are,' agreed her husband. 'I'm sure we made the right decision.'

Time passed by and one day a man's wife was out in the woods when she saw all the little rabbits scurrying about.

'I've never seen anything so exciting in my life,' she said to her husband enthusiastically. 'Wouldn't it be marvellous if we could have some little people?'

So the two of them went to see the god who made the world. He listened and then said the same to them as he had said to the rabbits. The man and his wife felt the same as the rabbits and, sure enough, there were soon boys and girls running round their home.

Now the people and the rabbits got real joy from their children, although they had to work hard to bring them up. They told them stories, they taught them how to do things and they watched them grow up. And as they got older themselves they still felt that they had made the right decision.

However, the stones in the world thought very differently.

'We don't want any children,' they said to themselves.

And so they never had any and they lived for ever and never died.

PRAYER

Let us pray this morning for parents of both people and animals. Let us give thanks for the way in which they take care of their young.

HYMN

'All the animals' No 80 *The Complete Come and Praise*

Information for the teacher

1. This is the sort of assembly which can be used for appropriate occasions when there is a need to focus on a particular parental theme, such as Mother's Day. It could also be used as sensitively as possible if there has been a bereavement in the school.

2. This story is an adaptation of a traditional Nigerian folk tale.

3. When thinking in terms such as 'the Maker' and 'the Creator', older children are often interested to learn that the *Qur'an* contains 'ninety-one beautiful names of Allah'. These cover a multitude of virtues, e.g. al-Hakim (the Wise) and al-Karim (the Generous).

4. An extremely relevant biblical reference is the famous words:
   'Everything that happens in this world happens at the time God chooses.
   He sets the time for birth and the time for death,
   the time for planting and the time for pulling up,
   the time for killing and the time for healing,
   the time for tearing down and the time for building.
   He sets the time for sorrow and the time for joy,
   the time for mourning and the time for dancing . . .
   He sets the time for finding and the time for losing,
   the time for saving and the time for throwing away,
   the time for tearing and the time for mending,
   the time for silence and the time for talk.
   (Ecclesiastes 3:1–7).

QUALITIES

27 KEEP CALM!

INTRODUCTION

When things go wrong it is often terribly difficult to keep calm, particularly if you are five years old! This morning's story is about a remarkable little girl who not only kept calm in a crisis but also . . . well, listen to the story.

STORY

Kimberley Wainwright was playing with her dolls on the dining-room table. Then she had a thought.

'I wonder what Mum and Gran are doing. They are very quiet.'

She went into the kitchen. There was nobody there. She looked out of the window into the garden. There was nobody there either.

'They must be upstairs,' she thought.

The five-year-old went upstairs and headed for her mother's bedroom. When she pushed the door open she got a terrible shock. Her mother was lying half on and half off the bed and her gran was lying on the floor beside her.

'Mum,' shouted Kimberley, 'Mum . . . Gran . . . wake up!'

Although she shouted loudly, and then shook both of the women, neither of them showed the slightest sign of waking up.

'They must be ill,' thought Kimberley. 'They might die!'

She was very frightened indeed, but she realised that she must get some help immediately.

'I'll go next door,' she said to herself.

She ran downstairs and went to the back door. It was locked and the keys were in the door. Climbing on a chair she reached them but she couldn't turn the key to unlock the door. She looked at the glass panels of the door.

'There's only one thing to do. I'll have to break the glass and crawl through.'

But no matter how hard she hit the glass she couldn't break it enough to crawl through. Only a tiny hole and crack appeared.

She noticed the telephone, quickly picked it up and dialled '999'. When the emergency services answered, she asked them to send an ambulance and she even remembered the exact address to tell them.

Kimberley then sat down at the bottom of the stairs to wait. It wasn't very long before she heard the siren of the approaching ambulance. She heard it stop and the footsteps of its crew hurrying up to the front door. As one of them reached to ring the bell, Kimberley called out.

'The door's locked but if you wait I'll get the keys out of the lock and put them through the letter-box for you.'

Then she climbed up on the chair again, took the keys out of the lock, pushed them through the letter-box and moved the chair out of the way. The ambulance crew came in and one of them knelt down beside Kimberley.

'Don't worry. We'll have everything sorted out in no time. Now just show us where your mum is.'

In no time at all the two women were being treated and helped to recover and it was all thanks to five-year-old Kimberley.

PRAYER

Dear God, we give thanks that there are so many people who will help us when we are ill. Thank you for giving them their courage, calmness and skill. We also give thanks for the special qualities of so many children. Amen.

HYMN

'One more step' No 47 *The Complete Come and Praise*

Information for the teacher

1. Mrs Wainwright had collapsed after suffering a suspected attack of vertigo and Mrs Brown, her mother, had fainted whilst trying to revive her. Mrs Brown later said that Kimberley had never even been taught how to dial '999' but must have seen it on television. An ambulance control officer said, 'It is amazing that a little girl of this age could act so wisely. She could well have saved her mother's life.'

2. For sources of further information on Royal Society for the Prevention of Accidents, see p 196.

3. A useful quotation might be: 'Keep calm when trouble comes' (Ecclesiasticus 2:2).

4. Warn children of the dangers of breaking glass.

---

28 WHY?

INTRODUCTION

Why are some people good at football? Why are others terrific singers? Why are some people so good at maths? Why are others good at art? The answer to these questions is that we don't really know. Because we don't really know, many storytellers have created tales with their own ideas about such things. We are going to hear a story like this today.

STORY

Ananse was very good at looking and listening. Wherever he went he kept his eyes and his ears wide open.

'It's a funny thing,' he said to himself, 'but lots of different people are clever in different ways. Now, if I collected all the things that people say and kept them, why, I'd be the cleverest of them all.'

So Ananse got the biggest hollow shell of a pumpkin that he could find.

'I'm going to call this my common sense jar,' he thought. 'And I'm going to fill it to the brim with common sense. Then there won't be much left for anybody else and I'll be the smartest one around.'

So for a very long time Ananse went about collecting common sense. He packed away every bit of it in his pumpkin shell until it was full to the brim.

'Now,' he thought, 'I'm going to hide this calabash [that is the proper name for a pumpkin shell] at the top of a very tall tree. Then I might use it to be the wisest person in the world or I might sell it a bit at a time and get very rich.'

So he started to climb a really tall tree, with the calabash round his neck. He climbed up and up. It was terrifically hot and the calabash kept bumping up and down and bouncing and bobbing round his neck.

'This is very irritating,' thought Ananse.

Then, out of the corner of his eye, he saw a small boy standing far below at the foot of the tree.

'What are you doing, Ananse?' called the boy.

Ananse ignored him.

'Ananse, what are you doing?'

Ananse went on climbing, becoming hotter and more irritated as he went.

'Ananse, why are you climbing that tree with a calabash round your neck?'

Ananse was furious.

'Will you get away . . .' he began, when the calabash slipped over his head. He tried desperately to catch it in his free hand, but it was no use. The great shell fell down and down until it smashed into a thousand pieces on the ground.

Now, at that moment, a sudden strong wind blew through the trees. It swirled over the broken calabash and began to blow the common sense in all directions. The wind continued to blow the common sense to lots and lots of different people. Everybody got some of it, but nobody got all of it. And that is how the world came to be like it is today.

PRAYER

Let us think this morning about the many things in this world which remain a mystery to us all. To help us to do this we are going to listen to, and think about, a very short poem.

'Poems are made by fools like me but only God can make a tree'.

HYMN

'The best gift' No 59 *The Complete Come and Praise*

Information for the teacher

1. The poem in the prayer was written by Joyce Kilmer.

2. The Ananse stories, which stem from Africa and the Caribbean, are famous worldwide. Ananse, the spider, is a trickster who is at the same time lazy and extremely clever.

3. A popular primary school RE theme is 'awe'. It is obviously appropriate when considering the many things in the world which people do not really understand. It is only a short step from this story to considering other 'mysteries'.

29 I REMEMBER YOU

INTRODUCTION

Kindness brings its own reward, often when we least expect it. This morning's story is about a man who thought he was certain to be killed until . . .

STORY

Paul was desperate.

'I can't go on much longer,' he thought, 'I've just got to find somewhere where I can rest and get my strength back.'

Then, through the blurring rain, he saw the dark opening of a cave in the mountainside.

'At last,' he said to himself. 'After a few hours sleep I'll be ready to move on again.'

Paul staggered into the cave and dropped exhausted onto the ground. Before his eyes closed, however, he thought of the last few hours. For several years he had been a slave, labouring without reward for a cruel master. Then, unexpectedly, there had been a chance to escape. He had taken it quickly and, running desperately through the countryside, he had tried to get as far away from his master's estate as he could.

'They'll be looking for me,' he thought as his weary bones ached and throbbed, 'and if they catch me there will only be one end.'

Slaves who escaped and were recaptured faced certain death.

Eventually Paul's eyes could stay open no longer and he fell into a deep sleep. He had no idea how long he slept, but when he awoke he was aware that there was something in the cave with him!

Keeping as still as he could he opened one eye carefully. There, standing over him was a huge lion! Stifling the scream which arose in his throat, Paul waited for the lion to attack him. But he was shocked. Far from snarling in anger, the lion whined piteously and held out a swollen inflamed paw for him to inspect.

Moving as slowly as he could, Paul tenderly took the paw in his hands. There, sticking in the bottom part of the creature's foot was an enormous thorn.

'You poor thing,' muttered Paul, 'that must really hurt.'

Being as careful as he possibly could, Paul gently eased the great thorn out of the tender foot. Then he bathed the paw with some water from a pool outside the cave. He finished the job by tearing a strip from his shirt and bandaging the whole foot.

Over the next few days the recovering man and beast helped each other. Then, with his strength regained, Paul set out once more.

Alas, within a day he was recognised, recaptured and taken in chains to his master.

'Ah,' snarled the cruel master, 'we're going to make an example of you. No slave will ever try to escape again when they see what happens to you.'

After being beaten, Paul was flung into a dark cell. There he lay until one morning he was dragged out by two guards.

'What now?' he gasped.

'You're going on a journey,' smirked the guard. 'And you won't be making a return trip.'

Paul was taken to the arena. This was a huge outdoor stadium packed with spectators. They had come to watch condemned men being thrown to the lions who ate them.

Soon a terrified Paul found himself being hurled onto the rough, bloodstained ground of the arena. A great roar went up from the crowd. Then there was a clang as a barred gate was lifted and a starved lion lurched hungrily into the stadium.

Paul closed his eyes and waited for the end as the great creature bounded towards him. Then, the roar of the crowd was stilled. Paul felt the hot breath of the lion above him and the wetness of its tongue as it licked his face! He opened his eyes and saw his old friend from the cave!

Once again the crowd roared. This time twice as loud for this was an amazing and unusual sight. Then the governor of the town stood up. After what he had seen, he ordered that both Paul and the lion be given their freedom.

PRAYER
Let us pray this morning that we have the strength and ability to give help whenever and wherever it is needed. Let us try to remember those famous words: 'Give and do not count the cost'.

HYMN
'Lost and found' No 57 *The Complete Come and Praise*

Information for the teacher
1. This is very much the sort of story which lends itself to impromptu drama, and a suitable presentation linked to the telling of the tale can be arranged and prepared within a few minutes.

2. No assembly presenter should ever be without a copy of *Aesop's Fables*. The more comprehensive the collection, the greater the source material for appropriate presentations.

3. One version of this story claims that it was St Jerome who took the thorn from the lion's foot. In consequence, the creature became the saint's faithful friend. In Christian art, the lion is a symbol of strength, majesty, courage and fortitude.

4. The winged lion is the emblem of St Mark and, therefore, also of Venice because this was the city under his protection.

30 A GOOD FRIEND?

INTRODUCTION
All of us have said to ourselves at some time, 'That's not fair!'

To feel unfairly treated is something which is very hurtful. When you have listened to this morning's story you'll probably all want to say something when it ends.

STORY
Peter lived at the bottom of the hill in a tiny cottage. He earned his living by mending shoes. But so few people lived near by that he hadn't many customers. This meant he was extremely poor. His pride and joy was his beautiful garden of flowers. He had no wife or children and, in a way, his flowers took their place.

At the top of the hill lived Herbert. He was a miller and was big, strong and rich. He had a wife and children and lived very comfortably. Whenever he came down the hill in summer he called in to see Peter and have a rest!

'Peter my friend, how are you?' he would say in a very loud voice. 'It must be good having a friend to drop in and see you like this.'

'Oh yes,' Peter would reply. 'Would you like a cool drink, Herbert?'

'I would indeed.'

The miller never refused.

Then when he was returning, before he went up the hill, he would drop in again.

'Hello Peter,' he would bellow, 'wonderful flowers you've got out there.'

'They are lovely, aren't they? Would you like some for your wife?'

'Certainly, certainly.'

The miller never refused!

So all through the summer months Herbert was a regular visitor at Peter's cottage. He had litres of cool, refreshing drinks and he took away hundreds of flowers. But he never actually brought anything.

'Don't want to embarrass him,' he would say to his wife.

'Well, why don't we ask Peter to come for a meal sometime?'

This was another suggestion from his wife.

'No, no, you should see the dump he lives in. When he saw how warm and comfortable it is here he'd be either embarrassed or envious. That wouldn't do at all. Oh no, no.'

When it was winter and icy winds blew, Herbert stayed in the warmth of his big house. He let other people do his fetching and carrying. He never dreamt of going to visit Peter.

Now one winter was particularly hard for Peter. He couldn't make any money and was desperately short of food. He had to sell everything he could think of to make ends meet. At long last, however, spring came and on the first really fine day, Herbert appeared.

'Oh I'm out of practice walking,' he gasped. 'I'm ready for drink after coming down that hill.'

'Sorry, Herbert,' replied Peter. 'I'm delighted to see you but I haven't got anything to drink. In fact it's been such a hard winter that I've got practically nothing.'

'What?' gasped Herbert. 'No drinks. You'll be telling me that you're not going to grow any flowers next.'

'You're probably right. I had to sell my wheelbarrow and I've . . .'

'Just a minute, just a minute,' interrupted Herbert. 'What are friends for? I've got a wheelbarrow I'll let you have. I'll bring it down one day.'

'Oh Herbert, how kind. That would be marvellous,' gasped the grateful Peter.

Now what had really happened was this. Herbert had just got a brand new wheelbarrow. His old one was cluttering the place up and he had to get rid of it. He hadn't been able to think what to do with it until . . .

'Well, as I say,' he said, slapping Peter on the back, 'what are friends for?'

All through that summer Herbert was an even more regular visitor at Peter's. Not only did he have more drinks and take more flowers, but he also asked Peter to do more and more things for him.

'Don't forget,' he would say, 'I'm going to give you my wheelbarrow.'

Of course he could never be bothered to bring it down the hill. But Peter, kind, innocent Peter, always thought, 'What a kind gift that will be when . . .'

Winter came again. Its icy hand gripped the hill and one night, with snow swirling in the strong winds, there was a thunderous knocking on Peter's door.

'Herbert!' gasped the astonished Peter when he opened the door.

'Listen, I need your help quickly. My wife is ill and we need the doctor immediately. Go and get him for me, will you?'

'But . . .'

The doctor lived six miles away and Peter was now old and frail.

'But Herbert . . .' he began again.

'I've got that wheelbarrow ready to bring down.'

'Very well, I'll do my best,' sighed Peter.

So poor Peter trudged six miles through the thickening snow. He reached the doctor's and passed on the message. The doctor galloped off on his horse. An exhausted Peter set off to walk back. He was almost in sight of his little cottage when he could go no further.

And so, there in the freezing snow, he died.

PRAYER
Let us think this morning of two things – friends and promises. Please God give us the strength never to break a promise and the qualities to be a worthy friend.

HYMN
'God has promised' No 31 *The Complete Come and Praise*

Information for the teacher
1. This is the sort of story which usually provokes a response from the children. Unfairness and injustice are commodities they feel strongly about, as all teachers know! The assembly presenter could decide whether the children's responses would be followed up in the hall or later in classrooms.

2. Many teachers will recognise this story as an adaptation of one of Oscar Wilde's originals. Most children now know his wonderful tale of the selfish giant. A beautiful book which contains both of these stories and four others as well is: Oscar Wilde and P. J. Lynch (illus.), *Stories for Children* (Simon and Schuster, 1991).

---

31 ONE GOOD TURN DESERVES ANOTHER

INTRODUCTION
Help someone else and you may find that later you are helped yourself. This morning's story gives us a reminder of this saying.

STORY
There was once a princess who lived in a very tall castle. The turret at the top of this castle had twelve windows and by looking through these one at a time the princess could see everything in the world.

Now many young men wanted to marry the princess but, to be considered, each had to pass a test to show that he was as clever as she was. The test was that they had to hide and, if the princess found them, they had failed.

They hid everywhere they could think of – in woods, down holes, in barns – but by looking through one of her twelve wonderful windows the princess could always see them.

Then one day along came Tom. He was young but wise and, before he hid, he spoke to the princess.

'Your highness,' he said politely, ' everyone knows how clever you are so I must ask for some help to match you.'

'Help you,' said the princess, 'what do you mean?'

'Well,' replied Tom, 'I need one day to think before I hide.'

The princess agreed.

Tom decided to spend his thinking day out in the woods. As he walked along he noticed a movement behind some bushes. Looking behind them he saw a fox crouching on the ground.

'Don't shoot, don't shoot!' cried the fox.

'I'm not going to shoot,' answered Tom calmly. 'I haven't even got a gun. But what's the matter? Why are you lying here?'

'I've got a terrible pain in my leg,' replied the fox, 'and I can't walk.'

'Let's see what we can do to help,' smiled Tom.

Now, because he was a country boy, Tom knew a lot about animals. After half an hour's stroking, pulling and twisting, the fox's injury was almost better.

When he had finished the fox smiled too. He felt better and he was the craftiest creature in the forest.

'Come with me,' he said, 'and trust me completely.'

The fox took Tom to a magic spring he knew. There, he dipped the young man into the water and turned him into – a hair-slide! Next he turned himself into a merchant and then he went, with the hair clip, to a market which he knew the princess visited.

Sure enough when she came the next day, the princess could not resist buying the beautiful hair-slide. On her way back to the castle, she realised that this was also the day when she had to look to see where Tom was hiding.

First of all she sat down in front of her mirror and fixed her attractive new hair-slide in place. Then she wandered over to the twelve wonderful windows. Looking carefully through each one at a time, she was astonished when, at the end of all twelve, she had seen nothing. This had never happened before.

'Where on earth can he be?' she wondered as she leaned far out of the last window.

As she did so the hair-slide slipped from her hair and sailed down to land on the ground below.

No sooner had this happened than the fox, who was waiting there in his proper form, sprang out, picked up the hair-slide and raced back to the magic spring with it. Once under the water Tom reverted to his normal shape too.

And so, as a young man, he went back to the castle and presented himself to the princess.

She admitted that she hadn't been able to find him. Secretly pleased, because he was such a charming young man, the princess agreed to her part of the bargain. A great ceremony was held and the two were married.

Now Tom remained good friends with the fox. One day when the two were out together Tom asked the question which had been on his mind.

'How did you work out that hiding place?' he asked.

The fox smiled.

'Well, think about it,' he said. 'Nobody can see out of the back of their head, so where better place to hide than in the back of someone's head?'

And he was right.

PRAYER

This morning we have heard an amusing story, but it does remind us of an important point. Never mind about rewards. If we can help someone then we should always do so as fully as we possibly can. Amen.

HYMN

'Cross over the road' No 70 *The Complete Come and Praise*

Information for the teacher

1. The idea for this story comes from *The Sea Hare* by the Brothers Grimm. The original is a much longer, more complicated tale and is different in many respects. As such it is not really suitable for assembly but it is nevertheless a good story for classroom use. It is dramatic and has a powerful message.

2. This is another of those stories where some ad libbed drama can be done more or less on the spot.

---

32 APPEARANCES

INTRODUCTION

Imagine that you go into an old-fashioned shop. On one of the shelves is a row of bottles. None of the bottles has a label on it but each one is filled with a different coloured liquid. Some of the colours are brilliant reds and greens, others are a dull grey or brown.

'Some of the liquids taste wonderful and are good for you,' says the shopkeeper. 'Others are very dangerous.'

But can you tell which do these things by just looking at them? Of course not . . . now listen to this morning's story.

STORY

This is a story about two men. One was called Egbert and the name of the other was Lancelot.

Egbert was a very vain man. He always dressed in the finest clothes and walked in a haughty manner. He was careful who he spoke to and he ignored anybody he thought wasn't worthy of his company. One of Egbert's great hobbies was walking. By himself, with his pack on his back, he would stride out through the countryside. He scorned any walkers he saw who weren't wearing proper walking clothes and boots.

One day he was out on a long and tricky walk. It started to rain heavily. Egbert had his waterproofs and he put them on quickly and fastened them tightly. The rain, however, had made the ground slippery and as Egbert strode along he slipped on the wet turf. He felt a sharp pain in his ankle.

'Aaah,' he gasped.

He was well-equipped with bandages and plasters but this needed something more.

'I've sprained my ankle,' Egbert thought to himself. 'I'm never going to be able to walk the five miles home. I'm going to need some help.'

Even as he was muttering to himself the rain stopped completely and, in clearing skies, he saw a large house about half a kilometre away.

'I'm sure the owner will help me,' Egbert thought.

And so he hobbled towards the large and imposing house.

'Hmm, somebody important must live here.'

For some reason, this thought pleased Egbert.

As he slowly got nearer he saw the front door open and a man came out. He was dressed in an old sweater, his trousers were tied with string just beneath the knees, his boots looked old and worn and he had a battered cap on his head.

'Must be a servant, or maybe the gardener,' thought Egbert as he staggered nearer.

The other man, whose name was Lancelot, looked up at the approaching stranger. He could tell by the look on his face and the heavy limp that the newcomer was in a lot of pain.

'Can I help you?' Lancelot called out in a concerned voice.

Egbert looked at the figure in front of him, taking in the old clothes.

'Yes,' he said in an important voice despite the pain he was feeling. 'Is your master in? Please go and get him for me.'

For a long while Lancelot looked at Egbert. But Egbert gazed into the distance as if Lancelot wasn't there. Finally, without another word, Lancelot put down the spade he was carrying, turned and went into the house.

He was away for quite a long time but eventually Egbert saw a figure come out of the front door. He smiled to himself. In just a glance he had taken in that the figure was wearing a smart, dark grey suit, a white shirt and a red and blue striped tie. On his feet a pair of black shoes gleamed and his hair was combed neatly.

Egbert fixed an important smile on his face and waited for the figure to approach him and then the well-dressed man stood right in front of him.

'Well, now can I help you?'

It was Lancelot!

For a minute, Egbert was speechless. Then his face turned a very deep red with embarrassment.

'Forgive my manners,' he said in a small voice. 'And yes, I do need help.'

'Then you shall have it,' smiled Lancelot.

Putting his arm round the injured stranger, he helped him through the garden gate and led him indoors.

Egbert had learned a very important lesson. He never judged anyone by their appearance again.

PRAYER
Let us never judge people on what they look like. Help us to remember the old saying: 'It is not what the bottle looks like that counts, it is what is inside it.'

HYMN
'Guess how I feel?' No 89 *The Complete Come and Praise*

Information for the teacher
1. There are many stories and anecdotes about not judging by appearances but this one is adapted from a true incident which happened to William Heath Robinson, the eccentric who gained fame as the propagator of ridiculous inventions and spawned the comment – 'that's a Heath Robinson effort.'

2. The word 'Sikh' means 'disciple' and the word 'Guru' means 'teacher' or 'leader'. One of the great Sikh leaders was a guru called Guru Gobind Singh. He wrote some useful words in the context of this story:
'All men are the same even though they look different,
The light and the dark, the ugly and the beautiful,
All human beings have the same eyes and the same ears' (Sikhism).

---

33 TWO BAGS FULL

INTRODUCTION
Look at the person sitting or standing next to you in assembly. Don't say anything but think about these questions. What are this person's good points? What are this person's bad points? Now, I wonder what they are thinking about you? This morning's story might make us think even more about these things.

STORY
Tien Chi was always complaining.

'I couldn't get on at school today because Rashid was talking every bit of the time.

Miss Evans is a really boring teacher.

Dakshina takes so long to get ready for PE that we miss half the lesson.'

These were the sort of comments he made to his mother after every day at school.

'I wish he wouldn't moan so much,' Tien Chi's mother said to his father one night. 'He's always finding fault with other people.'

'Well, his grandad's coming to stay with us this weekend. You know how wise he is. Perhaps he can stop Tien Chi from being such a misery.'

So, on Saturday when Tien Chi's grandad came, the two of them went out to watch a football match in the park. It didn't take long for Tien Chi to get going.

'That striker's not much good is he, Grandad? Oh dear, the goalie should have saved that dead easy. This ref's useless.'

After the match the two of them were walking home.

'You know, Tien Chi,' began Grandad, 'it is a pleasure and a surprise to see you standing up straight when you're walking.'

Tien Chi was puzzled.

'What do you mean, Grandad?'

'Well, haven't you heard of the two bags?'

'No.'

'Ah, well, there's a very old tale which says that each of us is born with two bags. We carry one of them in front of us and this one is full of our friends' and neighbours' and everybody else's faults. And then we carry one behind us and this one is full of our own faults.'

'Um,' muttered an increasingly thoughtful Tien Chi.

'So you see,' went on grandad, 'from the way you talk I would have thought you would be bent forward when you walk because your front bag was so much heavier than the one on your back.'

Tien Chi didn't say anything. In fact he didn't say much for the rest of the day. But he did do an awful lot of thinking.

PRAYER
Dear God, Teach us to be tolerant of the faults of others and help us to be aware of and do something about our own faults. Amen.

HYMN
'God knows me' No 15 *The Complete Come and Praise*

Information for the teacher
1. This might be a useful assembly when an issue such as bullying is being considered in a school policy.

2. A useful link here might be the story about the makers of Persian carpets. They are Muslim and are so aware that no human is ever perfect that they always make one small, deliberate mistake in every carpet they make. This is in accordance with their belief that only Allah can make anything perfect.

3. Finally, there are some useful quotations which could be linked to this story:
   'Stupid people always think they are right. Wise people listen to advice' (Proverbs 12:15).
   'The fault of others is easily seen, our own is difficult to see,' from the *Dhammapada*.
   'Remember silence is sometimes the best answer' (Tibetan saying).

34 DETERMINATION

INTRODUCTION
There is an old saying 'If at first you don't succeed then try, try and try again'. This morning's story shows you exactly what it means.

STORY
Savitri was desperately sad. She was very rich Indian princess who had married Satyavan. Satyavan was a wonderful husband who looked after his blind parents as well as her. But at the wedding a wise man had told the king, Savitri's father, that Satyavan would die in a year's time. The year was almost up.

The couple were in the forest. Through the canopy above them the sun streamed down. It was very hot.

'I've got a terrible headache,' groaned Satyavan.

'Come,' replied Savitri, 'sit here under this banyan tree and keep cool.'

It was no good. Satyavan's headache became worse and worse and then Savitri heard a terrible sound. The pounding of hooves told her that Yamraj, the king of the underworld, was riding towards them on his water-buffalo. He was coming to take Satyavan away from her!

'Banyan tree, please keep my husband cool underneath your leaves. I will come back for him as soon as I can.'

No sooner had Savitri said this to the tree than Yamraj arrived and swept away Satyavan's soul. But Savitri wasn't giving up that easily. She began to run after the god.

After a few kilometres he stopped and turned round.

'What is it woman? Why are you following me?'

'I can't live without my husband. Either give me his soul back or take me as well.'

Yamraj ignored her words and continued on his way. Still Savitri followed. Soon the irritated god stopped again.

'Look,' he said, 'it's no good, but I can see you are a determined woman. So, I'm going to give you one wish. But don't ask for your husband's soul back because that's the one wish I won't grant you.'

'Thank you,' bowed Savitri. 'Could my husband's parents be given their sight back please? That is my wish because I would so like them to be able to see again.'

Yamraj snapped his fingers.

'It's done,' he said. 'Now go home and don't bother me anymore.'

But Savitri continued to follow the god.

After another burst of speed, Yamraj hauled his pounding water-buffalo to a stop again.

'All right, all right,' snapped the exasperated god. 'Look I'll give you one more wish if you'll stop following me. One more – that's all. And of course it cannot be for the return of your husband's soul.'

'You're so kind, my lord,' muttered Savitri. 'Please could my husband's father have his lost kingdom back? That would make him so happy. To think of him being able to see again and once more to be king – that would be wonderful.'

This time Yamraj clapped his hands.

'It's done,' he said. 'Now, goodbye.'

In a swirl of dust, god and water-buffalo swept away again. But there, dogged as ever, was Savitri, following as always.

Yamraj couldn't believe his eyes when he looked round and saw his pursuer still there.

Once again he stopped. He was furious.

'Right!' he said. 'I'm giving you one final wish and warning. This has got to stop!'

'My lord, could there ever be anyone as kind as you?' said Savitri, bowing low. 'Could I please be the mother of sons? That is my wish.'

'Yes. Yes. It's granted,' called the god impatiently. 'Now go!'

But despite everything, Savitri still followed.

Eventually Yamraj stopped again.

'Please,' he said pleadingly. 'Please stop following me. I've given you three wishes. I can do no more. Why are you still following me?'

'Well, my lord,' Savitri began hesitantly, 'you see . . . you said I could be the mother of sons. But you have my husband so my sons can't have a father so your last wish is no good and . . .'

'Stop! Stop!' The god looked up at the sky and then dropped his arms by his sides. 'I've had enough of you. I can't take any more. Here, have your husband's soul back.'

And so Savitri hurried back to the banyan tree. There Satyavan's soul was reunited with his body. He yawned as she reached him.

'Oh, I must have been asleep,' he mumbled, 'and, do you know, I feel quite well again.'

And so the couple went on to live a long and happy life together.

PRAYER

Let us pray this morning that if we are ever in trouble we have someone as determined as Savitri to help us. Let us pray for all those people who spend their working lives helping others. Amen.

HYMN

'From the darkness came light' No 29 *The Complete Come and Praise*

Information for the teacher

Indian myths and legends offer great scope for assembly material. A much longer version of this old Indian tale and several others are contained in Madhur Jaffrey's *Seasons of Splendour* (Puffin, 1992).

---

35 RIVER RESCUE

INTRODUCTION

One of the silliest acts that some people do is to break things, just for the sake of breaking them. Sometimes this is more than silly, it is really dangerous. You'll see that when you listen to this morning's story.

STORY

Police Constable Kevin Hood ran along the bank of the River Wear.

'Hello,' he shouted. 'Can you hear me?'

There was no answer from the woman in the river. She had fallen in from a high bridge and was obviously hurt. But PC Hood knew from his lifeguard training that you had to try to get the attention of somebody in trouble in water.

'Hello,' he shouted again, this time even louder. 'Can you hear me?'

Again there was no reply from the woman.

'She must be unconscious,' thought the policeman. 'I'll have to go in and get her. But first I need a lifebelt to see how strong the current is and as something for her to hold on to.'

Kevin was a very good swimmer and he was confident he could help the poor woman but he definitely needed a lifebelt.

In the distance he saw a lifebelt holder and raced towards it. When he reached it he was shocked. The lifebelt had been ripped off and was gone.

Quickly he dashed towards the next holder he could see in the distance. This time the lifebelt was there but its rope was completely tangled. Still keeping watch on the woman who was floating ever faster downstream, the policeman desperately set about untangling the rope.

Finally he managed it and threw the lifebelt into the river. As soon as he saw how fast the current was flowing he plunged in after it and swam towards the woman.

'You're going to be all right. Don't worry,' he gasped as he got near her.

She was not unconscious but was in shock and couldn't speak. But when Kevin got the lifebelt beside her she was able to take a grip on it.

Then, with the rope wrapped round one of his powerful arms, the brave policeman began to swim for the shore. Hanging on to the lifebelt with all her strength, the injured woman was towed along behind him.

When the two reached the river bank, passers-by pulled them out and a waiting ambulance sped them both to hospital. The injured woman had to stay in hospital for treatment but PC Hood was allowed to go home after a check-up.

'I've had to help people like this once or twice before,' said the brave policeman, 'but I would ask people never to touch lifebelts unless they need them. It makes rescue much more difficult if there isn't a lifebelt around when you need one.'

PRAYER
Let us pray this morning that people are given the sense to realise that it is dangerous to play with, or damage, life-saving equipment. Let us all be aware that lives could be lost if we do foolish acts like this.

HYMN
'He who would valiant be' No 44 *The Complete Come and Praise*

Information for the teacher
1. This incident took place on the River Wear in Sunderland in August, 1999. PC Hood had been a swimming pool lifeguard for eleven years before joining the police force.

2. Two topics for further discussion are the consequences of vandalism and the dangers of water. In connection with the latter, some comment concerning the Water Safety Code might be useful. For sources of further information, see p 196.

---

36 'LET'S GET REALLY RICH!'

INTRODUCTION
I expect that sometimes you'd like to stay up later at night to watch more television; or you'd like just a little bit more of that delicious birthday cake; or you want a bigger bike; or . . . well, just listen to the story and think.

STORY
The day Jacob and his wife Maria found the goose they couldn't believe their luck.

'It can't belong to anybody out here,' muttered Jacob.

'But how could it have got here?' asked Maria worriedly.

'Never mind about that,' replied Jacob. 'Now we've got a goose and that means delicious eggs.'

Jacob and Maria lived in a tiny cottage in the woods and they were desperately poor. Jacob worked long hours as a woodcutter but some days there was barely enough to eat. So finding the goose was a wonderful stroke of luck and just how wonderful they were soon to find out!

Having found an old wooden crate for the goose to live in, Jacob went out to see it next morning. As he approached it, the goose got up and waddled off. Something glistened in the straw.

Jacob drew closer, then . . .

'Maria!'

Maria got such a shock at his yell that she dropped a jug of water and rushed out to see what was the matter.

'Maria! Look!'

Jacob pointed at the straw. It was an egg that glittered there. But this was no ordinary egg.

'It's . . . it's gold.'

Jacob's voice was just a whisper as he said this. Maria stretched out a cautious finger and touched the egg.

'You're right – it is gold,' she breathed.

The poor couple couldn't believe their luck. For most of the day they kept looking at and touching the golden egg. Tomorrow they would go to market and they would get things they never dreamed they could afford.

And so the next morning they got up early and prepared to make the journey to the market. Before leaving, Jacob went out to check on the goose and there lay another fresh golden egg!

So Jacob and Maria's lives changed completely. Every morning a new golden egg awaited them. They now wore splendid clothes, ate the finest food and their cottage was as warm and comfortable as it could possibly be. Jacob and Maria didn't bother working any more.

One night the couple sat talking.

'I suppose there'll be another golden egg tomorrow,' said Jacob.

'Yes,' replied Maria, 'it's a pity she doesn't lay two at a time. We could do a lot more with two gold eggs a day.'

'You're right,' agreed Jacob. 'In fact if we didn't have to wait and we had a whole lot of eggs together we wouldn't have any worries at all. We could get everything we want all in one go.'

'Well then,' interrupted Maria, 'why don't we . . .'

'Yes,' snapped Jacob. 'We'll kill the goose and take all the eggs out at once.'

So they killed the goose. But they found when they had done so that it was just like any other goose. There were no golden eggs inside and now it couldn't lay any more for them either.

PRAYER

Let us think this morning about being content. Let us be grateful for those things which we have got. Let us not be discontented and want more. Let us never be envious of other people.

HYMN

'I come like a beggar' No 90 *The Complete Come and Praise*

Information for the teacher

1. Ecclesiasticus 5:1 provides a salutary quotation in connection with this assembly: 'Do not rely on money to make you independent'.

2. A different approach to the same theme can be found in George Eliot's *Silas Marner*. The good thing about this story as an example for children is that a happy ending ensues when the miser loses his hoard and then establishes other values.

37 A DIFFERENT KIND OF HERO

INTRODUCTION

During wars many terrible things happen and medals are often given to people who perform heroic acts in difficult and dangerous circumstances. In this morning's assembly, however, we are going to hear a war story with a difference. No medals are awarded in this story but it is certainly one to make us think.

STORY

The weather in the North Atlantic was very cold. A moaning wind swept waves harshly against the sides of the Dutch ship as it wallowed on its journey. The date was 1940 and the Second World War had begun only a few months earlier.

Below the sea's troubled surface, conditions were very different. Inside the submarine there was the hum of the motors and it was warm and stuffy. The boat eased its way through the depths. This was the German submarine U-60.

'Up periscope,' commanded the captain, Adelbert Schnee.

Like a spear shooting upwards, the periscope fizzed upwards until it cleared the surface of the sea. As the water streamed from it, Captain Schnee's eyes fixed once more on the slow-moving ship.

'Target moving nearer,' he called out. 'Prepare to fire torpedoes one, two and three.'

In another part of the submarine other members of the crew prepared the giant torpedoes for firing. Then the captain's urgent voice snapped another order.

'Fire one . . . fire two . . . fire three.'

There was a lurch in the submarine as the torpedoes left it and hissed their way through the water towards their target.

Meanwhile, aboard the Dutch ship, the crew were going about their duties as usual. Some were on duty, some were eating their supper and others were asleep in their bunks before going on watch.

The sudden explosion sent a wave of shock, damage and noise through the ship. It was followed by a second and a third explosion. The great ship slowed, and then began to settle in the water.

'Abandon ship!'

The order boomed out throughout the doomed ship and men, hurriedly pulling on their lifejackets, began to run for the lifeboats.

Beneath the surface, still looking through his periscope, Captain Schnee watched the ship sinking and the lifeboats pulling away from it. Above all, he felt a great sense of sadness.

'A fine ship going to the bottom,' he thought. 'My orders are to sink all enemy ships but at least I can do something to help those poor men in the lifeboats.'

'Prepare to surface.'

At the captain's order, the submarine began to rise slowly upwards. And so, with water streaming from the casing, it broke the surface. Their were cries from the men in the boats.

'Look! There's the U-boat that sank us!'

'He's come to finish us off.'

'Get down quickly! He's going to open fire.'

Then the hatch of the submarine opened and the white-capped figure of the captain appeared.

'I'm sorry I had to sink your ship, but if you take the bearing I'm going to give you it will take you towards one of your vessels which is quite near. I'm going to pass over what supplies we can spare too. Good luck, fellow seamen.'

Then two members of the U-boat's crew threw some supplies to the lifeboats. When this was done, the sinister shape slid once more beneath the sea. The men in the boats gazed at where it had been.

'He must be a brave man,' said one of the survivors. 'He must have known that there were other ships racing here to attack him.'

'Yes,' replied another, 'and he took the time to try to help us as much as he could.'

It was not long before the survivors were picked up.

PRAYER
Let us pray this morning for the end of all wars. Help us Lord in our own school to value friendship and concern, to help others and to avoid arguments, bullying and making fun of others. Remind us yet again that we must treat others as we would like to be treated ourselves.

HYMN
'Peace, perfect peace' No 53 *The Complete Come and Praise*

Information for the teacher
1. Adelbert Schnee survived the war. Another story concerning him claims that he actually had a British cruiser, HMS *Belfast*, in his periscope sights when the order to surrender came. Without hesitation, he let the great ship go. It now lies in the Thames where it is a great tourist attraction.

2. Comment might be made about the Red Cross Organisation which exists to help in war, regardless of which side the recipients of its help are on. Jean-Henri Dunant, born on 8th May 1828, was the founder of the International Committee of the Red Cross. He was the first winner of the Nobel Peace Prize in 1901 which he shared with Frédéric Passy. For sources of further information, see p 195.

38 GIVE A LITTLE THOUGHT

INTRODUCTION

There are times when we are all thoughtless with regard to other people. How do they feel? What do they want to do? We don't think about these questions because we are too busy thinking of ourselves. Think about this while you listen to this morning's story.

STORY

Ali was a thoughtless man. He wasn't cruel or mean, just thoughtless. He lived in a very hot country and his most valuable companion was his donkey. Without it he couldn't carry things to market to sell or bring back the food he then bought. But he never thought about how his donkey felt.

'I wonder if I'll see old Abdul today? I'm looking forward to having some of that new wine I've got. Perhaps the Wazir's daughter will buy from me today.'

These were the sort of thoughts which were always buzzing through Ali's head. He never wondered if his poor donkey was hungry, thirsty, tired or neglected.

One day Ali was on his way to market. Trailing along behind him, at the end of a rope, was his donkey. On their way the two of them passed Wasim, the wise man.

'That donkey looks exhausted,' thought Wasim. 'It's time that Ali was taught a lesson.'

Wasim followed the pair. Ali was dreaming as usual and he didn't notice when Wasim slipped the halter off the donkey's neck and put it on his own.

Still holding his end of the rope, the unsuspecting Ali walked on for nearly a mile. Then, with a great yawn, he happened to glance over his shoulder.

'What the . . . ?' he shrieked in amazement. 'But what . . . how? Wasim! You . . . here. Where's the donkey? How?'

'Look at me, Ali,' said Wasim. 'Would you give me a drink and some food?'

'But of course,' replied the confused Ali, 'but . . .'

'Ah', went on Ali, 'but how long since you'd given your poor donkey a drink and some food?'

'Well, last night I'm sure. At least I think it was last night. I'm not really sure, but I must have done.'

'That's not good enough, Ali. Your donkey is your faithful servant and companion. You should remember that always.'

Ali was filled with shame at his thoughtlessness. The two men turned and went back to where the donkey was still waiting patiently.

When Ali saw him more terrible feelings of guilt swept over him. He turned once again to the wise man.

'Thank you, Wasim,' he said. 'You've taught me a very important lesson today.'

PRAYER

Dear God, Help us to think of others. Help us not to attach too much importance to ourselves. Teach us the value of sharing that precious thing called time. Amen.

HYMN

'I listen and I listen' No 60 *The Complete Come and Praise*

Information for the teacher

1. This is a very free adaptation of a story from *The Arabian Nights*. Many tales from this source are not really suitable for assembly but the idea of Scheherazade telling a nightly cliffhanger to preserve her life is a useful one to follow up. Children will certainly recognise the quality of a person who has the ability to beguile them with wonderful stories.

2. Before leaving this topic it is worth mentioning that, for teachers who want to take the Arabian nights theme further, a beautiful compilation of them is Brian Alderson's *The Arabian Nights* (Victor Gollancz, 1992). This book has outstanding illustrations by Michael Foreman. Finally, the music from *Scheherazade* is outstandlingly good for many assembly moods.

3. A useful Buddhist quotation in connection with this story is: 'All that we are is the result of our thoughts'.

---

39 FORGIVENESS

INTRODUCTION

There is a very old saying 'to err is human, to forgive divine'. What it means is that all of us make mistakes some time and we are very grateful when we are forgiven for making them! This morning's story is an unusual one of how somebody was forgiven.

STORY

Haroun was a man who owned a tobacco plantation. He made a living by selling the tobacco. No one was quite sure how he managed to make a living because in so many ways he was a stupid and stubborn man.

One day he realised that he needed to stock up on food. He went out and rounded up his one-eyed donkey.

'Now,' he said to the donkey, 'I'm going to load you up with tobacco. Then you are to go to Abdulla's shop. Tell him to sell the tobacco and then, with the money he gets, he should buy all the food I need for three weeks. He is to load all that onto your back and then you are to bring it straight home.'

Now, of course, we know that a donkey couldn't possibly understand a message like that! And naturally this donkey was no different from any other. So you see what we mean about Haroun being a bit, well, stupid!

Anyway, the donkey set off down the mountain road. He hadn't gone far before he met another traveller. When this man saw the donkey's load he couldn't believe his eyes.

'A stray donkey with no owner and all that stuff on its back. This is my lucky day!'

So, this rather dishonest traveller simply kept the donkey and all its goods for himself.

Meanwhile Haroun waited for a few days for the donkey to return. When it didn't he became impatient and angry.

'He's taken off with all that food for himself,' he thought. 'I must go and find him.'

First he went to Abdulla's shop. When he got there he was rude and loud and accused Abdulla of all sorts of dishonesty. Of course Abdulla had never even seen the one-eyed donkey that week so Haroun's accusations made him understandably angry. However, he decided he would get his own back by playing a trick on the stupid Haroun.

'Oh yes,' he said. 'Now I remember your donkey coming in. Yes indeed. He told me he was going to Baghdad.'

'Baghdad!' shouted Haroun. 'How dare he and with all my food too.'

So the furious Haroun immediately set off for Baghdad. Once he got there he began pestering everybody he met about his donkey. Now one of the men he shouted at was a great practical joker. He listened carefully to Haroun's story and then he looked very serious. Stroking his chin, he spoke in a most concerned way.

'Oh yes, that donkey. Well you know he's turned himself into a man. And what's more that man is an important judge.'

This of course was absolute nonsense but, by an amazing coincidence, there was a judge in the city who had only one eye. Haroun found out about this. When he had done so he went to the market and bought some grain. Then he went to the judge's house.

'Could I see the judge, please. It is most important.'

When the judge came out, Haroun looked at him without saying anything. Then he put his hand into his pocket and held out a handful of grain.

'Right, you can turn back into being a donkey again now. You're going home!'

The judge looked at Haroun as if he was completely mad.

'Leave my house at once,' he commanded.

At this Haroun lost his temper and began to beat the judge with his stick. The noise and shouting brought the servants rushing out and they grabbed the angry Haroun. When everybody had calmed down, the judge, who was a very wise man, decided he had better get to the bottom of the mystery. He asked Haroun to tell him the whole story.

Everybody was absolutely amazed when they heard it and they realised that Haroun was about the silliest man they had ever known. However, after a pause the judge spoke calmly.

'Lots of people have played some very unpleasant tricks on you, my friend,' he said. 'I'm sure you didn't mean to behave towards me as you have. I am going to give you five hundred gold coins, which I think is what the donkey and its load was worth. Now I want you to go home and live in peace.'

PRAYER
Dear God, We thank you for helping people to forgive all the mistakes we make. Help us also to be patient and tolerant when others don't behave as we would like them to. Teach us also to laugh with people and never at them.

HYMN
'The King of love' No 54 *The Complete Come and Praise*

Information for the teacher
1. A useful quotation here might be: 'Stupid people always think they are right. Wise people listen to advice' (Proverbs 12:15).

2. A wonderful and more serious story of forgiveness concerns Elizabeth Fry, the eighteenth century prison reformer. She was staying in a hotel in Bristol. On returning to her room one night she saw a burglar hiding under the bed. With great composure, she knelt by the bed and began praying aloud asking for help for the burglar. Hearing this he shamefacedly came out and she asked him to sit down and discuss his problems with her.

---

40 'COME AND LIVE WITH ME'

INTRODUCTION
You will certainly know somebody who is very kind. Today we are going to hear about a young woman who thought she could help children and then went on doing it in a special way for a whole lifetime.

STORY
Lillian stood on the deck of the ship and looked towards the land which was slowly coming into sight on the horizon.

'I wonder what it will be like,' she thought. 'It will certainly be hot enough!'

She was right there because the ship was approaching Egypt. Lillian had grown up in a comfortable home in Florida, in the USA, but when she reached her twenties she decided she wanted to do something useful in a developing country where many people needed help.

So Lillian landed in Egypt. She had very little money with her and her first task was to find somewhere to live. Eventually she found a small house in a town called Assiut. The rent was cheap enough that she could just afford it because the house was so small.

'Now,' she said to herself, 'I must learn the language. If I'm going to live and work here, and be of some use, I've got to be able to talk to everybody.'

This wasn't easy but she worked hard and made new friends when she was doing so. Soon after this, one of her Egyptian friends came to see her. He looked very sad.

'I'm afraid I've got a sad story to tell you. There's a woman I know who is dying. She has no husband and her little baby girl, who is only a few weeks old, is going to be left all alone in the world. There is just nobody to look after her.'

'That's terrible,' said Lillian. 'I must go and see them.'

She did this and she and the dying mother became close friends.

'Will you . . . will you look after my baby for me?' the mother asked one day.

'Of course I will,' agreed Lillian, pushing the hair back from the sick woman's forehead.

So, when the mother died, she took the baby to live in her small house. Soon after this she heard of some baby twins who were in exactly the same situation. She didn't hesitate.

'I'll see if I can help them too,' she said to her friends.

This time she borrowed a donkey, collected the twins and brought them to her home.

Two years later, she still had the donkey but by now she had eight children!

Of course there were problems. Lillian still had very little money and sometimes this caused her a great deal of worry.

'If I don't get some money by next week, we'll have nothing to eat.'

She thought this several times and yet, amazingly, something always turned up to solve the difficulty. This was because people, not only in Egypt but also all over the world, began to hear about the marvellous work she was doing. When they did so, many sent her gifts of goods and money. These came from Egypt, the USA and Scotland.

The years went by and Lillian's 'house' continued to grow. Eventually it became an orphanage with lots of bedrooms, a bakery, a schoolroom and a chapel. It was spread over a large area and, over the years, more than six thousand Egyptian orphan children called it 'home'.

PRAYER

Let us give thanks this morning for the kindness of so many people in the world. Let us think particularly of those who care for children who have no parents or homes of their own.

HYMN

'The family of Man' No 69 *The Complete Come and Praise*

Information for the teacher

1. Lillian Trasher was twenty-three when she went to Egypt. She became famous all over Egypt and she was know as 'Mama Lillian, the Nile Mother'.

2. Links with other philanthropists like Dr Barnardo and Lord Shaftesbury could extend the theme of this story. For sources of further information see p 194.

3. A useful quotation here might be: 'Be always humble, gentle and patient. Show your love by being tolerant with one another' (Ephesians 4:2).

41 'I'LL STAY'

INTRODUCTION
This morning's story is about an exceptional young man. In a very dangerous situation he showed great courage. Try to imagine what it was like as you listen to the story.

STORY
One of the most important members of a helicopter's crew is the winchman. It is their job to go down on a rope and make sure injured people can be lifted into the helicopter and taken to safety. Ray Martin was a winchman.

'Come on! Your crew is ordered to take off.'

The sergeant shouted the message to Ray Martin.

'But the skipper said that one helicopter had already gone.'

'Yes and it's come back. The conditions were so bad that they couldn't get anywhere near the boat.'

As Ray Martin ran out to his helicopter the pouring rain lashed into his face and the raging wind nearly tore him off his feet. What weather to be out in a boat!

Ray was eighteen and he had only been in the Royal Air Force for five months.

'I hope I don't let anybody down on this trip,' he thought to himself.

With a roar, the helicopter thundered into the stormy skies. Its mission was to rescue a couple onboard a yacht who had been caught in the terrible gale off the coast. The yacht was drifting helplessly and in danger of capsizing any minute.

The crew searched the pounding seas beneath them. Then there was a cry from the pilot.

'There they are! Winchman, get ready to go down.'

Ray looked down at the frightening scene below. He was nervous. Then, steeling himself not to hear the screaming wind as it tore past the open side of the helicopter, he began his descent.

He lowered himself nearer to the heaving boat. Swaying and jerking in the wind, he wondered if he could get his feet onto the yacht and then, with a jarring thud, he made it. He saw immediately that he had landed in a very serious situation.

The yachtsman was lying unconscious in the bottom of the nearly swamped boat. His terrified wife was hanging on to him desperately.

'He hit his head. He's been like this for ages,' she cried.

'Right,' said Ray, making a quick decision. 'He needs to be taken to a doctor quickly.'

Signalling the helicopter, Ray then lifted the injured man into a harness and watched him be pulled up to safety.

'But what about us?' asked the man's tearful wife.

'Don't worry, I'll stay with you until the helicopter gets back.'

Ray was no sailor but he knew he had to look after the woman and hope the yacht would stay afloat a bit longer.

The helicopter roared away to the mainland and the two people on the yacht held on to each other as it tossed in the dreadful sea. By the time the helicopter returned, things were getting desperate. The yacht was sinking fast and Ray was completely exhausted.

'Don't worry,' he gasped, 'we'll make it.'

And make it they did – just – as the boat sank the minute they reached the safety of the helicopter.

Now, apart from being very brave, Ray was also a very modest young man. He didn't bother to tell his family and friends how he had saved two lives. But they found out when a newspaper announced a few months later: 'Young National Service Airman Wins George Medal.'

PRAYER
Dear God, Give us the strength to do our very best when we are asked to do something for others. Help us to use as fully as we can the gifts of our minds and bodies.

HYMN
'Travel on' No 42 *The Complete Come and Praise*

Information for the teacher
1. For many years after the Second World War, young men of eighteen were conscripted to serve in the armed forces. This compulsory service varied in length from eighteen months to two years.

2. Deeds which earn medals provide many inspiring assembly stories. This is also true of accounts of the brave animals who have been awarded the Dickin Medal.

---

42 PROMISES, PROMISES

INTRODUCTION

'I'm going to take you to a football match tomorrow.'

'We're going to get a new TV for your bedroom.'

'We're going on a lovely holiday next week.'

These are all promises and they are the sort of promises which make us feel excited because we feel certain they are going to come true. A broken promise is . . . well, listen to this morning's story.

STORY

It was a cold, frosty day in January 1749. A crowd of people jostled each other outside the Haymarket Theatre in London.

'What does it say?' called someone from the back.

'Something special is going to happen here on the sixteenth,' called a short man at the front of the crowd.

He was reading from a notice which was stuck on to the wall of the theatre. It said:

'YOU CAN'T MISS THIS!

16th January, 1749 – BE HERE!

On this day I will bring my walking-stick to this theatre. This is no ordinary walking-stick as you will see. IT IS MAGIC! I am going to play the sound of every musical instrument on this walking-stick. Then, at the end of the show, I am going to squeeze myself into a quart bottle.

DON'T MISS THIS FANTASTIC SHOW. YOU WON'T BELIEVE YOUR EYES!

Signed: The Magician.'

'He can't do that.'

'I don't believe it.'

'I'd like to see him try though.'

'Me too. We can't afford to miss this.'

These were the sorts of things which everybody was saying and, naturally, there was great rush to buy tickets for the show.

Eventually January 16th arrived and the streets round the Haymarket Theatre were packed with crowds. They were all going to see the most fantastic show ever!

Laughing and joking they pushed into the theatre and took their seats.

'I can hardly wait.'

'I wonder what he looks like.'

'Do you think he can really do it?'

In eager anticipation the audience waited . . . and waited . . . and waited.

'He's not coming.'

'We've been swindled!'

'We want our money back.'

The crowd's shouts got more and more angry. But the 'magician', who had promised to do such wonderful things, never turned up.

PRAYER

Let us think this morning about promises. Let us think about how terribly disappointed we are if our mums, dads, relatives and friends make promises to us and then don't keep them. Let us pray that we always have the reliability and honesty to keep any promise we make. Amen.

HYMN

'In the bustle of the city' No 101 *The Complete Come and Praise*

Information for the teacher

1. The result of the 'broken promises' of the story was that there was a riot and the theatre was completely wrecked.

2. The 'promise' in this story was of course a fraud and the children will enjoy hearing about one of the greatest con artists of all time, a man called Arthur Ferguson. In 1924, he made several 'sales' to American tourists: Big Ben for £1,000; Nelson's Column for £6,000; and a down payment of £2,000 for Buckingham Palace.

3. With regard to false promises made via advertising, in 1923 it was said: 'Appeal to reason in your advertising and you appeal to about four percent of the human race'.

4. For the full impact of this assembly, it is necessary to move from anything frivolous to a more serious consideration of promises. Useful quotations in this context are:
   'Whoever is faithful in small matters will be faithful in large ones; whoever is dishonest in small matters will be dishonest in large ones' (Luke 16:10).
   'Don't be quick to speak or lazy and negligent in your work' (Ecclesiasticus 4:29).
   'For God's promise was made to you and your children, and to all who are far away' (Acts 2:39 in which Peter's Pentecost sermon declares that this is God's promise to all who repent).

---

43 QUICK-THINKING WOMEN

INTRODUCTION

Every day our roads become busier. There are more cars, buses and lorries travelling on them and everybody has to be very careful to avoid accidents. This morning we are going to hear about two quick-thinking women who saved terrible accidents from happening.

STORY

The National Express coach was racing along the motorway on its way from Merseyside to London. Tina McCall, the travel hostess on board, was sitting in the front seat looking at the passing scenery. The driver next to her, Mark Davies, kept his eyes on the road.

Suddenly the coach started to swerve slightly from side to side. Tina glanced at the driver in alarm and then got a dreadful shock.

'Mark, Mark!' she cried. 'What's the matter?'

The driver was slumped over the steering-wheel. He was obviously ill and no longer in control of the coach! Desperate action was needed. Tina leapt across the space between them and grabbed the steering-wheel. Unable to reach the pedals, she tried first of all to stop the vehicle swerving.

Ignoring the screams of the terrified passengers, she got the speeding coach back onto a straight path and then began to edge it towards the safety barrier. The bus lost speed as it scraped along the barrier and this gave Tina a chance to pull on the handbrake. Slowly the coach came to a stop on the hard shoulder of the road.

The story had a happy ending all round. The only person injured was Mark, the driver. He was taken to hospital but needed only a day's treatment. The rest of the passengers and Tina continued on their way to London when a relief coach arrived.

Everybody thought Tina was a heroine.

'She saved people from being hurt, or possibly killed,' said a policeman.

The other brave and quick-thinking woman was called Ellen and her adventure began when she was walking towards a hill.

'That's a bit odd,' thought Ellen. 'That bus doesn't seem to have anybody in it but I'm sure I saw it move.'

The empty bus was standing at the top of a hill and, as Ellen looked again, it definitely started to move down the hill!

'If that gets going down there there'll be a terrible accident,' thought Ellen as she began to run towards the runaway vehicle.

By now it was picking up speed and a breathless Ellen had to run very fast to reach the driver's door. Wrenching it open, she turned the steering-wheel so that the front wheels turned towards the kerb.

Bumping and banging, it slowed down and finally came to a stop. Reaching inside, Ellen yanked on the handbrake.

'It's a good job I used to drive a minibus,' thought Ellen. 'At least I knew what to do.'

PRAYER

Let us pray this morning for all those who use our busy roads. Let us give thanks for all who work hard to keep transport safe for passengers to use. Let us say together these words written by St Patrick:

May the strength of God steer us,
May the power of God keep us,
May the wisdom of God teach us,
May the hand of God protect us.
Amen.

HYMN

'In the bustle of the city' No 101 *The Complete Come and Praise*

Information for the teacher

1. The coach incident took place on the M42 near Solihull in the West Midlands. The driver became ill due to the effects of a virus. Ellen Maiden, a 46-year-old mother of three, stopped the runaway minibus at Habberley in Worcestershire.

2. A useful biblical reference is: 'Be prepared for times when you will be put to the test. Be sincere and determined. Keep calm when trouble comes' (Ecclesiasticus 2:1–2).

3. For sources of further information see p 196.

44 THE FISHERMAN'S STORY

INTRODUCTION

We all enjoy inviting people we know and like to our houses. But what about strangers, or people who seem very different to us?

STORY

This is the story of Manuel, a Spanish fisherman who lived long ago.

Manuel was good at his job. He caught the best fish and made a lot of money selling them. As a result of this, he lived in a nice little house overlooking the blue waters of the Mediterranean Sea. Manuel was also a naturally kind man.

'There are many people who aren't as fortunate as I am,' he used to say to himself.

And he did lots of things because he believed this. For instance every Christmas Day he went out into the town. He then took the poorest person he could find back to his house for a magnificent meal.

'I wonder who I'm going to find today,' he thought as he set off one Christmas morning.

The first person he saw was a Moor. The man was obviously a slave and he looked desperately thin and unhappy. But Manuel was unsure. For a start Moors were Muslims and many of them were pirates who killed and captured Spanish people. Everybody in Spain hated them.

The Manuel cleared his mind of such thoughts.

'Come my friend,' he said to the Moor, 'I'd be glad if you could come to my house and share my Christmas dinner with me.'

The Moor, who was called Hassan, could hardly believe his ears. Him – a slave – being invited to a Spanish house! He wondered if there was a catch.

But, of course, there was no catch and the two men had a wonderful day together. They had a lovely meal, then sat in front of a warm fire and chatted. Before he went, Manuel even gave his guest some warmer clothes to wear during the winter.

And so, at the end of a marvellous day, the slave went back to his master.

It wasn't many weeks after this that the fisherman heard that Hassan's family had a lot of money. When his family finally heard that he had been captured, they gave his owner a large amount of this money. As a result he was freed and went home.

And so the years passed by. To keep getting good fish Manuel began to seek his catch further and further out to sea. Then one day, disaster struck.

'Heave-to!'

The order rang across the water. It came from a Moorish pirate ship which had raced up to Manuel's boat.

Soon Manuel was in chains on board the pirate ship destined to be sold in the slave market in Algiers.

'To think I've come to this,' thought Manuel a few days later.

Tired, dirty and hungry, he stood in chains. He was waiting to be bought as a slave and spend the rest of his life in misery and hardship. Rich Moors walked past, looking him up and down as if he were an animal. One of the buyers stopped in front of Manuel and spoke sharply.

'I'll take this one,' he said.

Manuel paid no attention to this. After all what did it matter who bought him? It would all be the same.

Then he heard the buyer's voice again. This time it was much softer.

'You don't recognise me, do you?'

Manuel looked more closely at the man . . . and yes . . . it was Hassan, whom he had entertained to Christmas dinner all those years ago!

'I've never forgotten your kindness,' continued the now rich Hassan, 'and now here is a chance for me to do something for you.'

And so he arranged for Manuel to be freed and sent home to Spain.

PRAYER

Let us give thanks this morning for kindness, wherever and whenever we find it. Let us think particularly of those who show kindness to people less fortunate than themselves.

HYMN

'Lord of hopefulness' No 52 *The Complete Come and Praise*

Information for the teacher

1. This old Spanish tale has many similar counterparts from different cultures. An interesting book offering a good selection of folk stories is: Robert Ingpen and Barbara Hayes (illus.), *Folk Tales and Fables of Europe* (Dragon's World, 1992).

2. Fishermen and fish are significant in the Bible. The fish is a symbol of Christ because in Greek the five letters which make up the word 'fish' are the same initial letters of 'Jesus Christ, God's Son Saviour'.

45 THE BOASTFUL QUEEN

INTRODUCTION
Do you know anybody who is always telling you how good they are at something? I hope not. This morning's story is about a queen who was always boasting and the terrible event which came about because of it.

STORY
'It really is lovely, quite lovely.'

The woman who said this was a queen called Cassiopeia and she was talking about her own hair! Sitting in front of a long mirror she was brushing her long black hair and admiring it with every stroke.

Her husband Cepheus, King of Ethiopia, and several servants were around as she spoke.

'Don't you think it is lovely?' called Cassiopeia to Cepheus.

'Yes, my dear, very nice,' replied the king.

'And they say those Nereids are beautiful,' went on the queen, 'but I'm sure not one of them is as lovely as I am.'

Now this was a very dangerous thing to say. The Nereids were sea nymphs and one of the most beautiful of them was married to Poseidon, God of the Sea.

News of Cassiopeia's boast reached Poseidon's wife. She was very angry to hear this and complained to her husband. He was angrier still.

'Right,' he snapped, 'I'll put a stop to this!'

At once he sent an enormous sea serpent to the coast of Ethiopia.

'Cause as much trouble as you like,' ordered Poseidon. 'I'm going to teach that woman a lesson.'

So the huge sea serpent sank ships, drowned sailors and terrorised the whole coast. The people begged King Cepheus to do something about it.

Desperate, the king contacted Poseidon and pleaded with him to take the monster away.

But Poseidon had not forgotten Cassiopeia's boasting and he was in no mood to show mercy.

'Yes', he replied, 'I'll take the monster away, but there is a price to be paid.'

'Anything,' sighed Cepheus, 'anything at all.'

'You must chain your daughter to a rock and leave her there for the sea serpent.'

Now both Cepheus and Cassiopeia were distraught when they heard this.

'My darling daughter,' cried the queen. 'Oh how can I ever forgive myself for allowing this to happen?'

But, despite the tears and pleas, the price had to be paid. And so Princess Andromeda was chained to a rock in the restless waters off the coast. There, sobbing pitifully, she waited for the sea monster to come and claim her.

Now it so happened that at this time Perseus, a great Greek hero, was making his way home. He was flying over the sea using his magic winged sandals when he spotted the desperate princess chained to the rock.

'What's this?' he said to himself and then, in the churning waters, he saw the huge sea serpent approaching the rock.

Instantly Perseus hurled himself downward, drawing his sword as he did so. With a lightning blow, he killed the terrible creature just as it was about to tear Andromeda away from the rock. Then, with a massive blow from his sword, he cut the chain holding the princess to the rock. Sweeping her in his arms, he lifted her to safety above the hungry sea.

And so Perseus saved Andromeda and later they were married. But one thing you could be sure of was that Cassiopeia never ever boasted again!

PRAYER
Dear God, Help us to be modest at all times and to be grateful for any gifts or talents which have been given to us.

HYMN
'Somebody greater' No 5 *The Complete Come and Praise*

Information for the teacher
1. This is an adaptation of a Greek myth. A collection of such stories is a useful resource for assemblies.

2. Some of the older children may be interested to know that all the characters in this story appear as stars in the night sky. In the northern hemisphere, the constellation called Cassiopeia is easy to recognise because it looks like the letter 'W'.

CREATURES

46 KEEP YOUR WORD

INTRODUCTION

If you make a promise to someone you should keep it – anybody knows that. Sometimes, however, you make a promise when you have a problem and once the problem has gone away you don't feel the same way about keeping the promise. This morning's story tells about a promise made in worrying times.

STORY

Long, long ago in a hot country there lived many Native Americans and many animals. Unfortunately, in a great river in this country lived the Rainbow Snake.

He was called this because he had a magnificent skin which was made up of all the colours of the rainbow. Although he was incredibly beautiful, the Rainbow Snake was evil. When he surfaced from his river-bed home, it was to attack and eat anybody or anything passing by. The people and the animals were all terrified of him.

One day the chief called a great meeting.

'Now, my friends,' he said to all the animals and birds who had come to the meeting, 'it is time we did something about this dreadful Rainbow Snake. Anybody who kills him can have his skin for a reward.'

Now the Rainbow Snake's skin was so big and so lovely that anybody would have liked to own it. Even so none of the animals dared to say that they would attack the dreaded snake.

'Don't say you're all frightened!' snapped the chief, looking particularly at the biggest and fiercest of the animals.

'I'm not,' suddenly piped a small calm voice.

'Who said that?' asked the chief.

'Me.'

A sleek cormorant lifted his head as he spoke.

'I'm a good diver in water,' he went on. 'I think I might be able to dive down into the river holding an arrow in my mouth. Then I might be able to kill this terrible creature with the arrow.'

'Hmm,' muttered the chief doubtfully. 'Well it's worth a try and you know the reward for getting rid of this evil monster.'

So the cormorant got ready. With an arrow clasped firmly in his mouth, he plunged into the river. In the struggle which followed, the brave cormorant managed to kill the dreaded snake with his sharp arrow. Gasping, he got back to the surface and told the chief what had happened.

One of the men then dived into the river and tied a rope round the monster. Then, animals and people pulled the creature onto the land and skinned it. Soon the huge, gleaming skin lay shining brilliantly in the sun.

'I'll take my reward now,' said the cormorant, 'and I'm glad to have been able to get rid of this menace who killed so many of your people.'

The chief stroked his chin. Now that the snake was dead he didn't feel much like keeping his promise; now he wanted the skin for himself.

'I'll tell you what,' suggested the chief craftily, 'you can have it if you can carry it away.'

He hid a sly smile as he said this. After all the cormorant was tiny and the skin was huge; he'd never be able to carry it. The other people and animals began to smirk and smile behind their hands.

For a moment the cormorant was silent, then he threw back his head and gave a shrill cry. Within seconds the air was full of the sound of beating wings. Then, from every direction came dozens and dozens of birds. All pale and white they listened whilst the cormorant spoke.

'Friends,' he cried, 'please help me take away the skin of the Rainbow Snake.'

Immediately all the different birds clasped a piece of the skin in their beaks. Then, as one, they took off, carrying their splendid banner across the sky.

When they reached a safe place they landed. As they did so an amazing thing happened. The colours on the skin which each bird had carried suddenly transferred themselves to the feathers of the bird. And so, instead of being white anymore, the birds became red, green, blue and yellow and beautiful.

And from that day onwards the Native Americans, when they found a stray bird's feather, wore it in a band round their head. This reminded them of how the chief tried to break his promise.

PRAYER

Let us remember that whenever we make a promise it should be kept. Let us pray that we are always as reliable and trustworthy as we should be. Please God, help us to have these qualities in our day-to-day lives.

HYMN

'Who put the colours in the rainbow?' No 12 *The Complete Come and Praise*

Information for the teacher

1. This is an adaptation of an old Native American story. A well-known parallel of broken promises is the tale of *The Pied Piper of Hamelin*. This assembly could be supplemented by the reading of that story in its poetic form.

2. For those teachers who have the time and the inclination to search, a superbly illustrated hardback book retelling this story (PPH) was published in the late seventies by Blackie, written and illustrated by Joanna Troughton.

---

47 ONE DAY YOU MAY NEED HELP

INTRODUCTION
There is an old saying 'Pride goes before a fall'. This morning's story shows exactly what this means.

STORY
Archie was donkey who worked on a farm. He got all the hard dirty jobs but he never complained.

'What have I got to complain about?' he said to himself. 'I am well fed and although I have to work hard, nobody is cruel to me. It's not such a bad life.'

One day Archie was toiling along the road outside the farm. Two heavy sacks hung from either side of his tired body. Glancing up he saw a puff of dust in the distance ahead. As he watched, the swirling dust moved nearer and Archie saw that it was being thrown up by a magnificent horse. The horse was being ridden by a knight and both man and beast were handsome and beautifully groomed.

'Out of my way, peasant,' shouted the horse when he was still a long way off. 'Can't you see we're going to war. Move!'

Stumbling and staggering Archie got off the road as fast as he could. The charger thundered by.

'How I'd like to be him,' thought Archie. 'He's big, strong and handsome and he's going off to great adventures while I mess about here. I don't suppose he'll ever need any help from anybody!'

And so the weeks and months passed by. Winter came and one bitter day Archie met a friend of his who worked on the next farm.

'We've got a new helper,' said the friend.

'What, you mean another donkey?' asked Archie.

'No, a horse who was injured in battle and has been sent to work on our farm. Look, here he is coming now.'

Sure enough, coming towards the donkeys was an enormous cart. It was being pulled by a horse for whom every step seemed painful.

As he got nearer, Archie suddenly recognised him. The last time he had seen him he had been full of pride and self-importance.

'Perhaps he'd even be glad of my help now,' thought Archie.

PRAYER
Let us think this morning about how we treat people. Help us always to be polite and considerate and never conceited or unkind. Let us always be prepared to help others.

HYMN
'The earth is yours, O God' No 6 *The Complete Come and Praise*

Information for the teacher

1. This is a well-known tale from *Aesop's Fables*. They are a valuable source of good assembly material.

2. The relative positions of donkeys (asses) and horses in the Old Testament were quite polarised. Asses were burden carriers and indispensable farm workers. One of the reasons for this was that they ate only a quarter of what a horse did. Thus they were a far better economic proposition. In Solomon's time, the army contained '1,400 chariots and 12,000 cavalry horses' (1 Kings 10:26). This indicates the importance of the horse in military life. Jesus's use of an ass on Palm Sunday (John 12:14) became symbolic of both kingliness and humility.

48 HOME SWEET HOME

INTRODUCTION

This morning we are going to start with a quiz question. Which dogs live in tunnels? To find out for sure listen to this morning's story.

STORY

Tex and Wilma crouched in the tunnel just underneath the entrance hole to their village.

'Up you go,' said Wilma. 'It's your turn to be lookout.'

'See you later,' replied Tex as he scrambled up to the entrance. Built around this was a great mound of soil. Climbing inside this and putting his head out of the top, Tex could see far into the distance.

Tex, Wilma and the rest of their family were prairie dogs who lived in North America. They lived in their village which was part of hundreds of kilometres of tunnels. They didn't know all of the prairie dogs who lived in these tunnels and, therefore, every village had a mound at the entrance where a lookout kept guard.

'Well, I might as well get used to it. I'm here for a long time,' thought Tex as he settled down to his guard duty.

He looked out over the flat dusty land. He could hear the barking of other prairie dogs in the distance and this reminded him of a tale his grandfather used to tell.

Old Elmer had been very wise and knew about everything.

'Those two-legged creatures – you know, people – they call us prairie dogs because we bark like other dogs all over the world. But, of course, we don't look like dogs, we look like squirrels!'

Tex smiled at the thought of his grandfather. Whatever he looked like, or sounded like, he had a job to do. This was to guard his precious home and . . . then, Tex's whiskers twitched and he froze into complete stillness. A puff of dust caught his eye. It was getting nearer. Someone was coming!

A low growl started in Tex's throat as he got ready to warn the family and then, through the dust, he saw some very familiar features. It was Old Elmer returning from a trip on the plains.

With a bark of delight, Tex bounded out of the burrow and raced out to greet his grandfather. Putting their front legs on each other's shoulders the two prairie dogs rubbed noses as a greeting.

'Good to see you,' barked Tex.

'It's always nice to come home,' replied his grandfather.

PRAYER

Let us give thinks this morning for our homes and all who live in them. Let us be grateful for families and people who love and care for us.

HYMN

'For the beauty of the earth' No 11 *The Complete Come and Praise*

Information for the teacher

1. Prairie dogs are not dogs but a kind of ground squirrel. They are very cautious creatures who are suspicious of visitors from other districts in their vast network of tunnels. Consequently, they have guards on mounds. Any unwelcome visitor is driven off by a frenzy of barking whereas friends and family are greeted in the way described in the story.

2. Dogs are a very popular subject with children. Wonderful tales of dog heroism can be researched in stories of the Dickin Medal awards. The Dickin Medal is the animals' Victoria Cross and it was instituted by Maria Dickin in 1943.

3. A useful address concerning dogs is Battersea Dogs' Home (see p 195).

4. It is interesting to note that in the Old Testament, dogs were invariably mentioned in the context of scavengers yet, in Christian art, the dog is often a symbol of watchfulness and fidelity.

---

49 THE TURNCOAT

INTRODUCTION

To call somebody a turncoat is to insult them. This is because a turncoat is a person who always sides with whoever they think is going to win an argument. This can be a dangerous thing to do as you will hear from this morning's story.

STORY

There was a war on! But it was a strange war. The birds and the beasts were fighting to decide who were the most important creatures in the world.

The birds were having a meeting.

'Animals can't fly so we must win.'

'Some of us are very big and can carry animals away.'

'If we are in charge of the sky then we are the most important creatures around.'

One bird after another was giving its opinion. There, in amongst them, was a bat. He listened carefully and from what he heard he was sure the birds would win.

'Yes, yes,' he cried. 'It's an absolute certainty. The birds will win. There is no doubt about it. It's great to be on the winning side.'

The birds all looked to see who was making so much noise.

Later the same day the animals were having a meeting.

'We can't lose this war.'

'How could birds stand up to great creatures like elephants and lions?'

'Birds could never rule the land and, therefore, we must win.'

Now it so happened that the bat had been passing by when he noticed this meeting. Again he listened very carefully and he saw the huge strength of the lion, tiger, elephant, rhinoceros and others.

'I made a mistake before,' he thought to himself. 'The birds can't possibly win against the strength of these creatures. This is the side I want to be on!'

So he called out in a loud voice, 'You can't lose, animals. No birds are as strong as you. There's no doubt that you will rule the world.'

Now, shortly after this, both the birds and the beasts came to their senses.

'What on earth were we thinking about?' they pondered. 'There's plenty of room for birds and beasts in the world. There's no need at all to fight about it.'

When this decision was made neither the birds nor the beasts would have anything to do with the bat. To this day the bat is still an outcast from both.

PRAYER

Dear God, Help us to make our own decisions. Give us the strength to be loyal to our friends. Teach us to be reliable in all that we see or do.

HYMN

'All creatures of our God and King' No 7 *The Complete Come and Praise*

Information for the teacher

1. Loyalty to our friends in time of need is the theme of a Buddhist story taken from the *Jataka*. In this tale, an antelope is trapped by a hunter. A tortoise gnaws away the ropes of the trap and a woodpecker flaps her wings in the hunter's face. After various adventures, and thanks to all helping each other, all eventually escape safely.

2. A dictionary description is very succinct: 'Turncoat – one who goes over to the opposite side or party; a renegade'.

3. Proverbs offers a further pungent comment: 'Wise people will gain an honourable reputation, but stupid people will only add to their own disgrace' (Proverbs 3:35).

---

50 THE STATUE AND THE SWALLOW

INTRODUCTION

There is a well-known saying: 'It is better to give than to receive'. Everyone gets a very special feeling when they have done something really helpful for another person.

STORY

The statue of the prince was magnificent.

'It makes the town square look really important.'

'With all those jewels in it, it shows everybody that this town is very prosperous.'

'We don't have ordinary statues here.'

These were the sorts of things people said in the town. The liked looking at the jewels which served for eyes in the prince's head. They admired the precious stones which were set into the handle of his sword. And his crown was, like the rest of the statue, just magnificent.

Late one day a swallow stopped for a rest on his way to a hot country. Sitting beneath the feet of the statue, he fluffed his feathers and felt drops of water landing on his back.

'That's strange,' he thought. 'It definitely isn't raining but I did feel those drops. Where can they be coming from?'

Just as he thought this, two more drops of water landed on him. He looked up and then he got a shock. There, trickling down the cheeks of the magnificent statue from his jewelled eyes, ran two lines of tears.

'Why is a wonderful statue like you crying like this?' gasped the bird.

'Ah, my friend,' sighed the statue, 'when I was alive I lived in a palace, had a good time and saw only the good things of life. But now I am a statue and high up here I can look down right over the town and I see some very unhappy people.'

'But I'm not really sure I know what you mean,' replied the bird.

The statue gave another long sigh.

'Just a few streets away from here there lives a desperately poor woman. At the moment she has fallen into an exhausted sleep. A child is lying in a cot beside her. The child is very, very sick but the poor woman has no money to get a doctor.'

'That is really sad,' agreed the bird in a concerned voice, 'but what can you or I do about that.'

'By myself, I can do nothing,' continued the statue, 'and neither can you. But together we could do a lot.'

'How?'

'Well, if you peck one of the jewels out of my head, you could then fly to that house and leave the jewel for the woman to find when she wakes up.'

'I could,' replied the bird, 'but I'm resting. Tomorrow I have a very long flight ahead of me and if I don't get plenty of rest I won't be able to do it.'

The statue said nothing.

'Well,' continued the bird, 'you do see what I mean, don't you?'

Still the statue said nothing. There was a long pause and then, finally, the bird spoke again.

'All right, all right,' he said at last. 'I'll do it.'

And so, with snow falling round him, the swallow pecked a jewel from the statue's head and then flew with it to the poor woman's house. He left the jewel on the table next to where she was sleeping.

When he got back to the statue it was bitterly cold.

'How do you feel after that?' asked the statue.

'Strangely enough, despite the fact that is so cold and I need rest, I feel a real glow of warmth inside.'

PRAYER

Dear God, help us to help those in need even when we are tired or impatient or short of time. Let us remember that even a smile and a kind word are important gifts to those whose lives are troubled.

HYMN

'The best gift' No 59 *The Complete Come and Praise*

Information for the teacher

1. To a certain extent this story has been left 'up in the air' at its final point. As such, it is at a good point for discussion or elaboration. Alternatively, some teachers might want to finish the tale (what appears here is an excerpt from a longer Oscar Wilde tale) as the full story has a most poignant ending.

   The swallow remains in the cold town for the whole winter and eventually delivers all the prince's jewels to needy people. Finally, because he has not escaped to the warmer climate he needs for survival, the bird dies at the statue's feet. The townspeople see this and also the fact that the statue's jewels are all gone. As a result they think it is now not good enough for them and they have the statue knocked down. God sees all this and takes from the town its two most precious things: the body of the bird and the statue's leaden heart.

2. This story of helping others in need might be linked with tales from the *Jataka*, which is the 'birth story' of the Buddha and relates tales of his earlier lives.

---

51 RICKY'S STORY

INTRODUCTION

There are many stories of incredibly brave animals. This one is about Ricky, a Welsh sheepdog, who lived during the Second World War.

STORY

'Well, the poor little chap deserves a home.'

Mr Litchfield scratched the ears of the young sheepdog as he spoke.

'Ricky, so that's your name is it?'

The woman with tears in her eyes nodded. Her house had been bombed and now she was going to live with friends but they had no room for her dog, Ricky.

So Ricky went to live with Mr and Mrs Litchfield. It didn't take him long to settle in his new home and he soon showed that he was a rather special dog.

'Do you know, he's the brightest dog I've ever known,' said Mrs Litchfield one day.

'I agree,' smiled her husband, 'I sometimes think he's got more brains than me.'

Soon after this, Mr Litchfield read that the army were looking for intelligent dogs. He took Ricky along to them and within a few weeks the sheepdog was training to detect mines.

During the war, soldiers planted bombs in the ground. These bombs are called mines and they put them there to injure the enemy. Ricky was trained to sniff out mines so that his soldiers would come to no harm.

Ricky was working with the British army in Holland on 3rd December 1944.

'Come on, lads! This way,' shouted Sergeant Major Maurice Yielding, who was in charge of Ricky and some British soldiers. They were looking for German mines.

'I'm sure there are some along this canal bank,' muttered Sergeant Yielding, as he led the group forward. 'You lot wait a bit 'til I check it out.'

Slowly the sergeant got further and further ahead, until suddenly . . . BANG!

A mine went off near him.

Sergeant Yielding fell injured to the ground. A piece of shrapnel from the mine whistled past him and cut Ricky's ear.

'What are we going to do?' gasped one of the other soldiers.

'We've got to get the sarge back. He's badly hurt.'

But Ricky knew what he had to do.

Despite his bleeding ear, he crouched down and began to move forward. Sniffing carefully, he began to pick a path through the deadly mines. The rest of the men followed him, marking the path with tape as they did so.

Eventually they reached the injured sergeant and carried him back to safety.

Ricky was a hero. For his courage in saving a person's life, he was awarded the Dickin Medal, the animals' Victoria Cross.

PRAYER
Let us give thanks this morning for the courage which is needed to help people when they are in desperate need and danger. Let us value the intelligence, companionship and faithfulness of so many of our pets.

HYMN
'All the animals' No 80 *Come and Praise* Vol 2

Information for the teacher
1. There are two other tales about faithful dogs which might be used to follow up this assembly.
   The well-known Greyfriars Bobby story is retold in Lavinia Derwent's *The Tale of Greyfriars Bobby* (Puffin, 1985). This is the story of the dog who remained faithful to his Scottish master even after the man's death.
   Tobias was the dog owned by St Roch, a fourteenth century saint. When on a pilgrimage to Rome, Roch was caught in an outbreak of the plague. He went from place to place ministering to victims until he himself was stricken by the disease. It was then that Tobias saved his life by bringing him bread and water until he recovered.

2. In caring for and about our animals, Proverbs is pertinent: 'Good people take care of their animals, but wicked people are cruel to theirs' (Proverbs 12:10).

---

52 'THE CANARIES'

INTRODUCTION
Let's start this morning by thinking about football teams (questions and responses could follow here). Just about every football team has a nickname. Arsenal are called 'the Gunners', Sunderland are known as 'the Black Cats' and Southampton are nicknamed 'the Saints'. But one team's nickname has a particularly interesting history, as you will hear.

STORY
Norwich City are a famous football team. They play in green and yellow colours (the same colours as a certain bird). Before they went to play in their present stadium at Carrow Road, their ground was called 'the Nest'. Now, having heard all of these clues, you won't be surprised to know that their nickname is 'the Canaries'.

They got this name because, before 1912, Norwich was a great centre of canary breeding. These birds were kept by ordinary people who lived in the lower-lying part of the town. The birds lived in cages in their garden sheds.

Then, in August 1912, something drastic happened.

'Looks like rain today.'

All over the city people were saying the same thing on this dark and terribly overcast morning.

'More than looks like rain – here it comes.'

'Quick, let's get inside! This is the heaviest rain I've ever seen.'

'Must just be a very heavy shower.'

But it wasn't. From early on August 26th through to mid morning on August 27th there was a downpour such as nobody had ever seen before. Forty bridges were washed away; electricity and gas supplies were cut off; thousands of crops were destroyed; hundreds of homes were flooded; and all transport was stopped. Norwich was cut off from the outside world.

Thousands of people had to leave their homes with no time to take anything with them. There were huge queues for food and, lost in the chaos and panic, most of the canaries had drowned.

The canary breeding industry in Norwich never really recovered from this disaster. So, only by knowing a bit of history could you know why Norwich City Football Club is called 'the Canaries'.

If we think about this we can see that knowing something of the past helps us to understand much more about names today. For instance, Barnardos is the name given to an organisation which helps disadvantaged children. It gets its name from Dr Barnardo who first began to seek and care for abandoned boys and girls.

The Samaritans, who give people emotional support today, got their name because Jesus told the story of the good Samaritan who helped a man who had been robbed. Christians get their name because they believe in the way Jesus Christ taught people how to live and believe.

One thing we can be sure about is that finding out about the past is important!

PRAYER

Let us give thanks for all those great people who have lived in the past. By their courage, imagination, inventions, discoveries and concern they have made our lives today so fulfilling and much safer.

HYMN

'He's got the whole world' No 19 *The Complete Come and Praise*

Information for the teacher

1. Possible follow-up work could be based on the charities mentioned in this assembly. An alternative is to take the name 'heroes/heroines' and follow it up in a specific context. This might be rescue at sea to continuing the water theme. For sources of further information see pp 194, 196.

2. The biblical reference for the parable of the good Samaritan is Luke 10:25–37.

3. Finally, it is possible in discussion relating to floods that the story of Noah might arise. In this context the following poem could be used.

It surely did rain.

'The rain, it's a comin',' said the Lord.
Time for Noah to get the animals aboard.
Rain came down forty days and nights
Weren't no land in anybody's sights.

Twenty more days in the Ark a creakin',
Noah sent a raven land a seekin',
Back he came 'cos the place weren't dry
So three weeks more then another try.

This time success and the Ark was grounded
On Mount Ararat it foundered.
Next a rainbow its colours unfurled
And God said, 'All's right with the world.'

53 TOO CLEVER BY HALF

INTRODUCTION
This morning's story is about a monkey who thought he was much cleverer than anyone else. Where did his conceit get him? Listen and you will find out.

STORY
It was the thorn in his tail which started everything off.

'I must get it out,' thought the monkey. 'The man to see about this is the barber.'

So the monkey went to the barber and explained what he wanted. The barber was a kind man and tried to help immediately.

'I'll get it out with one of my razors,' he said. He began to prise away the thorn carefully. But no matter how careful he tried to be, he couldn't help cutting a bit of the monkey's tail as well.

Was the monkey grateful when the thorn was out? Not a bit!

'Look at my tail,' he snarled. 'Just look at that cut!'

'I'm sorry,' protested the barber, 'but after all the thorn is out, isn't it?'

'How dare you,' continued the monkey. 'Put that piece of tail back at once or give me your razor.'

Obviously the barber could not put the piece of tail back and he ended up giving the irate monkey his razor.

Feeling very pleased with himself, the monkey went on his way. Eventually he came across an old man cutting wood to make himself a fire.

'Here, you need some help,' the monkey said craftily. 'Use this razor, it is really sharp and will make a much better job of cutting.'

'Why thank you,' answered the old man, 'that's very kind of you.'

But the razor was really not strong enough for cutting wood and it soon broke. The monkey pretended to be absolutely furious.

'Now look what you've done,' he screamed. 'My lovely, special razor wrecked. You'll have to give me all your wood to make up for it.'

Sadly, the old man handed him the carefully cut pile of wood and the monkey went on his way again. Next he came to a tiny hut. Looking in, he saw a woman trying to cook a piece of meat on her fire. But it was obvious the fire was soon going to go out for lack of wood. The monkey shouted to the woman.

'You need some help, like more wood. Here, take mine.'

'Oh thank you, you are so kind,' replied the woman.

She piled the monkey's wood on the fire and soon delicious smells showed that the piece of meat was almost cooked.

'Just a minute,' exclaimed the monkey, as if an idea had just come into his head. 'You've used all my wood on that fire so it is only fair that I get all the meat.'

The poor, hungry woman, who had intended to share the meat with the monkey anyway, sadly handed over the whole lot.

'Aha, a good morning's work,' thought the monkey as he went on his way. 'Now I'm off home to have a real feast.'

However, the wonderful smell of the succulent cooked meat wafted through the forest to a pack of starving wild dogs. Bounding and snarling they chased after the smell and found the meat and the monkey. Having chased him up a tree, they ate every piece of the meat.

PRAYER
Help us never to be tempted to try to cheat other people because we think we are cleverer, bigger or stronger than they are. Give us too the ability to share gracefully at all times.

HYMN
'A still small voice' No 96 *The Complete Come and Praise*

Information for the teacher
1. This story is an adaptation of an old tale from Thailand. Like Indian stories, tales from this country often come from the Buddhist *Jataka*. These stories frequently contain characters who are monkeys, dogs, peacocks, elephants and jackals.

2. 'All that we are is the result of our thoughts,' is a useful Buddhist quotation.

3. In Christian art the ape often symbolises malice and cunning. Sometimes Satan is portrayed in the shape of an ape.

54 THE BULLFIGHTER

INTRODUCTION

When we think of bullfighters our thoughts turn to Spain, hot dusty days and swirling red cloaks. Nothing could be more different from the bullfighter you are going to hear about this morning.

STORY

His name was Rudiger von Stoer, but everybody called him Rudi. Rudi was a very small dog, a dachshund, and his owner was a man called Commander Mowatt. One morning the two of them were out walking.

'Steady on there,' called Commander Mowatt, 'we're meeting my friend Hugh here in a minute.'

'Not in a minute, I'm right behind you,' said a cheerful voice.

It belonged to Hugh Welch, Commander Mowatt's friend.

'I didn't want to be late,' went on Hugh, 'because I thought we might go up and visit the farm this morning.'

'Good idea,' agreed Commander Mowatt. 'It's been a while since we've been up there. Come on, let's go.'

So the three of them set off up a long, winding path which led through fields to a farm. When they were nearly there, Rudi got a stone caught in one of his paws.

'Just a minute and I'll get it out for you,' said Commander Mowatt.

He bent down to tend to the dog's paw and Mr Welch strolled on ahead. It took a little time to get the stone out but finally the job was done. Commander Mowatt was straightening up when he heard a desperate shout.

Looking up he saw a horrific sight. Mr Welch had been attacked by the biggest bull he had ever seen! As he watched, the commander saw his friend, who was a big strong man, seize the bull's horns to try to protect himself. But he was no match for the huge animal. With a contemptuous flick of its head it flung him in the air and then prepared to attack him as he lay on the ground.

'I'm coming, I'm coming,' yelled Commander Mowatt frantically as he ran to Mr Welch's aid.

But before he had gone ten metres something shot past him like a whizzing brown bullet. It was Rudi going to the rescue!

The little dog raced up to the bull snarling and snapping at the great creature's legs. For a moment the bull was distracted, then it decided that it must deal with this irritating little dog before it could finish off the man.

Bending its great head, the bull gored the tiny dog with its great horns. Still Rudi barked, snarled and snapped.

By now Commander Mowatt had reached the scene. He was helping Mr Welch to his feet when the bull turned, looked at the two of them and decided he had had enough. It galloped away with a snort.

The two men then ran over to the battered and bleeding Rudi. He was rushed to the vet's and after treatment he made a full recovery. Not only was he a hero but he also received a magnificent medal to prove it!

PRAYER
Let us give thanks this morning for all dogs. Let us remember not only the pleasure they give us as pets, but also the marvellous work they do as guide dogs for the blind and hearing dogs for the deaf.

HYMN
'He who would valiant be' No 44 *The Complete Come and Praise*

Information for the teacher
The training of guide dogs for the blind began in Germany in 1916. Useful organisations here are the Guide Dogs for the Blind Association and Hearing Dogs for the Deaf (see p 195).

55 THE EAGLE ON THE GATEPOST

INTRODUCTION
Some creatures are so fierce that it is thought they cannot be tamed. The golden eagle is such a creature and yet a girl once saw one sitting peacefully on a gatepost in Pwllheli. She set about finding its story.

STORY
'But why don't you use rifles to shoot the wolves which are attacking your sheep?'

The Englishman stroked his chin as he puzzled about this. He was putting the question to a local khan in Kirghizia, which at the time was a republic of Russia.

'Ah, to use rifles would lead to disaster, my friend. You see, the sound of a rifle shot could well set off an avalanche. That is why we have to use these eagles to kill the wolves.'

As he spoke the khan nodded towards the fine but savage-looking Berkut eagles.

'Hm,' replied the Englishman. 'Well you won't be using one of them for much longer if he doesn't get some urgent medical attention.'

A crafty look came over the khan's face.

'Perhaps you'd like to buy her from me then?' he asked, trying to hide a greedy look.

So the exchange deal was done and the eagle became the property of the Englishman. What he really wanted was for the creature to have its life saved. He found that the bird was suffering from a throat infection which was very serious. As soon as he could, he went to Pakistan and visited the university there. Fortunately they had a drug which cured the great bird.

'I'm going to call her Atalanta,' said the Englishman to himself, 'and wherever I go, she's going with me.'

He had a great deal of travelling to do but so kind had he been to this normally savage creature that she came to look upon him as a parent. So man and eagle became very fond of each other.

Eventually, in the 1960s, Atalanta arrived in Great Britain and her owner took her to live near the sea.

'There's nothing savage about her now,' he said. 'She'll fly to the near-by mountains but she always comes back home. And she's so tame that she's quite happy to let children stroke her. And this was once a bird used for killing wolves!

PRAYER

Let us think this morning about appearances. Atalanta looks fierce but is friendly and gentle. Let us not make the mistake of judging people by how they look and let us remember the value of kindness and care for others.

HYMN

'All creatures of our God and King' No 7 *The Complete Come and Praise*

Information for the teacher

1. The owner of this eagle was called Samuel Barnes. The species was once considered incredibly valuable and there is a story of how Richard the Lionheart exchanged three thousand falcons for one golden eagle which belonged to Saladin. At the time, only emperors were allowed to own these birds.

2. This story could be used in a wider theme considering the close bonds which can be developed between humans and animals. Such stories abound and regular checks in national and local newspapers can yield plenty of modern examples.

3. A further extension which relates well to this story, is a consideration of man's concern and help for animals in distress. For sources of further information see pp 195–196.

4. There was an early belief that the eagle's plumage never faded and that it stayed perpetually young by periodically flying near the sun and then plunging into water. Therefore, in Christian art, it came to symbolise resurrection and new life: 'He fills my life with good things, so that I stay young and strong like the eagle' (Psalms 103:5).

---

56 EVER BEEN HAD?

INTRODUCTION

Often when children are caught doing something naughty they offer excuses like 'I didn't think,' or 'they told me to'. This morning's story is a good reminder of how important it is to think before you act.

STORY

The weather was getting colder. There was a biting chill in the air which even the great lion felt as he stopped by the well. Then, hearing an unusual noise from the well he looked down into it. A wolf sat there.

'Wolf, hey wolf! What are you doing down there?'

'Ah, good morning, Mr Lion. Well, actually I'm making a sheepskin coat.'

'A sheepskin coat! Fantastic, just what's needed now it's getting cold. Will you make me one too?'

There was a long pause and then the wolf spoke again.

'Well,' he said slowly, as if deep in thought, 'it is very hard you know. For a start, you'll have to bring me the skins.'

'Oh, I'll bring you the skins all right. I'll start getting them now.'

So off went the lion to scour the countryside. Within a couple of hours he had caught two sheep. He brought them back to the well and threw them down.

'Wolf, here's some skins.'

'All right, that's a start. But you know you are a magnificent creature and it'll take plenty of skins to make a sheepskin coat for you.'

'How many will you need?'

'At least one or two every day that I am working on the coat.'

So the pattern was established. Every day the lion caught one or two sheep and threw them down to the wolf. After a week had gone by, the lion became impatient.

'Surely you've had enough skins by now? When is that coat going to be finished?'

'I reckon two or three more skins should do it.'

After four more lambs had gone down the well, the lion began to get really angry.

'I want that coat ready by tomorrow. It's getting cold now and I'm fed up with waiting for a warm coat.'

'Sir, I promise it will be quite ready for you tomorrow.'

But it wasn't!

'I've had a bit of a problem with some of the stitching,' sighed the wolf, 'but it's as good as finished now. Bring a rope tomorrow and we'll get it up to you.'

The next morning the lion arrived with a rope and lowered one end into the well. There was some scuffling at the bottom and then the wolf shouted.

'Pull!'

Now what the lion didn't know was that the wolf, who had grown very fat after eating all the sheep the lion had thrown down to him, had tied himself to the end of the rope.

The lion couldn't believe the weight he was having to pull up.

'This must be the best, heaviest, warmest sheepskin coat ever,' he thought to himself. He gave another great heave and suddenly the wolf burst out of the top of the well.

Throwing a couple of sheepskins at the lion to confuse him, the crafty creature bounded off with a great bark of laughter.

'Keep warm,' he called.

When the lion realised what had happened he was absolutely furious. 'To think I was as silly as that! No common sense at all.'

He couldn't stop thinking this for weeks.

PRAYER

This morning's prayer is a poem:

Give me common sense good Lord
Each day that I'm at school.
Keep my mind alert not bored
Don't let me look a fool.

A friend to others let me be,
One who is always there.
Knows the value of a smile,
And never fails to share.

HYMN

'One more step' No 47 *The Complete Come and Praise*

Information for the teacher

1. This story is an adaptation of a traditional tale from Iraq. Traditionally, storytellers called 'Qassakhoon' told their tales in coffee houses and would begin their stories with a short verse of Muslim philosophy. *Iraq Folk Tales* (Books and Books Ltd, 1995) is a very useful little book written by various authors in a most straightforward manner.

2. Muslim references to Allah can vary because the *Qur'an* contains 'ninety one beautiful names of Allah'. Examples are al-Hakim (the Wise) and al-Karim (the Generous).

3. Wolves have a great reputation for cunning but one was certainly outdone by a herdsman in Russia. This wolf was killing calves on a farm and the farmer played tapes of savage dogs barking to try to frighten it away. The wolf was not scared by these tapes but, when a tape of music was played, the wolf stopped to listen and was caught.

4. This quotation is one of the many biblical reminders about wisdom: 'Wise children make their fathers proud of them; foolish ones bring their mothers grief' (Proverbs 10:1).

---

57 THE STORY OF THE COWS

INTRODUCTION

If we are having fun, it is much better if we can share that fun with some-body else. It is the same if we are worried. Sharing our worries with a friend always helps. This morning's story shows just how important sticking together and sharing really is.

STORY

The wise man was very old. He knew he wasn't going to live much longer so he asked his three sons to come and see him.

'I want to tell them a story which will really make them think,' he said to himself.

So the three sons came to see their father.

'Now,' said the old man, 'you know that no cows live in the jungle any more, but do you know why?'

His sons shook their heads.

'Long ago,' continued their father, 'many cows lived in the jungle but so many of them were killed by lions that they moved out and asked peo-ple to look after them. There were three of them, however, who wouldn't move and they were never bothered by the other animals.'

'Why was this?' asked the eldest son.

'I'll get to that,' replied the old man. 'One of the cows was dark red and had fierce horns, one was pure white and had horns which were nearly as fierce. The third cow had no horns and because of this the other animals thought she had magic powers. No matter what happened, these three stuck together. If there was any trouble, they always solved it together.

Then one day a new lion arrived from another part of the jungle. He was cunning and patient. For more than a week he watched the three cows and then he came to a decision. He waited until the red cow was grazing a little way from the others. Hiding in the bushes, he spoke to her quietly.

"You are the most handsome cow I have ever seen," he whispered. "That red coat is magnificent. You shouldn't be wasting your time with those other two, you should be a queen. Nobody would ever bother you and absolutely everyone would look up and admire you."

The red cow was flattered and very pleased.

"A queen," she thought to herself.

"Don't worry," continued the lion. "I'll arrange it for you."

The next day he waited until the white cow was some distance from the others.

"I have never seen a cow so beautiful," he gasped. "White is such a wonderful colour. If you didn't have to bother with those other two you'd be a real princess of the jungle."

The white cow was delighted.

"He's right," she thought. "I am beautiful."

"Don't worry," continued the lion. "We'll talk some more about this."

A few days later the lion caught up with the cow without any horns.

"Oh, magic one," he called admiringly, "everyone has told me how incredibly clever you are. I'd be grateful if you could help me with a problem."

"A lion asking for help from a cow – that's really something!" thought the hornless cow. "I'll go and help him straightaway."

So the lion and the hornless cow went off into the jungle. As soon as they were completely out sight of the others, the lion leapt on the cow, killed her and ate her.

Meanwhile, the white cow was wondering what the lion was going to do about making her a princess.

"I must go and find him and ask how he's going to do it," she thought.

So she wandered off to look for him. He was waiting. Soon he had eaten her too.

Now, without her two friends to help her keep safe, the red cow was alone. The lion chose his time, then he killed and ate her too.'

When the three sons heard their father finish the story they all nodded and thanked him.

'Don't worry father,' they said, 'we will always stick together.'

PRAYER
Let us think this morning about our families and friends. Let us pray that we are always a loyal family member and a trusty friend. Let us pray too for those people who are lonely and alone in the world.

HYMN
'Join with us' No 30 *The Complete Come and Praise*

Information for the teacher
1. This is an adaptation of a traditional Kenyan folk tale.

2. A useful quotation might be: 'I will tell you about ten kinds of people that I feel fortunate to know . . . someone fortunate enough to have a real friend' (Ecclesiasticus 25:7–9).

58 HELP FROM THE BIRDS

INTRODUCTION

We all make mistakes in our lives and when we do we hope that other people will forgive us and try to help us. This morning's story comes from Japan and tells of some very unusual help.

STORY

Orihime was a princess. She was also very good at weaving clothes, but she wasn't very happy.

'My father makes me work so hard that I'll never get the chance to meet the man I'm going to marry,' she thought.

Orihime's father was Tentei, King of the Stars. His daughter made such beautiful clothes that he certainly kept her busy.

One day, however, Orihime took some time off from her weaving and met a young man. He was called Kengyu. The two fell in love.

'All right,' said Tentei when he heard about it, 'I'm very happy for you, my dear. You most certainly should get married, but you must never stop making the beautiful clothes you produce.'

So Orihime and Kengyu were married and were very happy. So happy, in fact, that Orihime forgot to work altogether.

One day her father came to her and saw the weaving loom standing covered in dust.

'I warned you that you must not stop working,' he told Orihime. 'Now you and Kengyu must live apart on either side of the river.'

Orihime was horrified. The river was the Milky Way which runs through the Kingdom of the Stars. There was no way to cross it unless the boatman of the moon came to ferry a passenger across.

Tentei knew this and, if he was feeling angry, he would cause it to rain so hard that the river would flood. Then it would be impossible for the boatman to come and do his ferrying.

Now all the magpies in Japan heard this sad story. So when the river was flooded and the boatman could not work, they did something about it. They all flew to the river and formed a bridge across it. Then Orihime tiptoed over their feathered backs to see her husband on the other side.

PRAYER

Dear God, Please help us to forgive people who do things to annoy us. Please help us not to make mistakes which cause problems for others. Let us also value the help of kind words and deeds. Amen.

HYMN

'He's got the whole world' No 19 *The Complete Come and Praise*

Information for the teacher

1. This is a fairly free adaptation of an old Japanese folk tale. The following title is an excellent collection of folk stories about the heavens with outstanding illustrations: Mary Hoffman and Jane Ray (illus.), *Sun, Moon and Stars* (Orion Children's Books, 1998).

2. Some useful quotations here might be:
   'He is best loved who does most good to other creatures' (Islam).
   'Happy are those who are merciful to others; God will be merciful to them' (Matthew 5:7).
   'If your brother sins rebuke him, and if he repents, forgive him. If he sins against you seven times in one day, and each time he comes to you saying, "I repent" you must forgive him' (Luke 17:3–4).

3. An interesting follow-up along the theme of 'we are all a mixture of good and not so good' is the reference to magpies in this story. In general, these birds have an unwelcome reputation (e.g. the thieving magpie) but in this story they appear in a much more admirable light.

59 WHO IS GOING TO DO IT?

INTRODUCTION
Most people have seen 'Tom and Jerry' cartoons on television. This morning's story is about cats and mice too. It starts with what seems to be a brilliant idea.

STORY
Behind the dusty skirting-board, the mice were all gathered together. There was an awful lot of angry whisker-twitching going on.
    'It's disgraceful!'
    'It's never been as bad as this before.'
    'We must do something about it.'
    'Yes. But what?'
    It seemed that everybody had something to say and they were all talking about the same thing. A new cat had come to live in the same house as all the mice. He was very cunning and was beginning to make their lives an absolute misery.
    Suddenly one important-looking mouse cleared his throat loudly.
    'Er . . .'
    The others looked at him expectantly.
    'I think I have the answer to our problem.'
    'Go on, go on,' called out the others excitedly.
    'Well, we must get a small bell. I know where I can get one. Then we must put the bell round the cat's neck. Then, wherever he goes, the bell will ring and warn us that he is around.

'Brilliant!'

'What a marvellous idea.'

'I think our friend should have some extra grain for coming up with such a marvellous idea.'

The important-looking mouse looked even more important. He tossed his head in the air and smiled at his cleverness and then a small voice interrupted all the congratulations.

'But . . . just a minute.'

The other mice looked to see who had spoken. It was one of the smallest of their number and he usually had little to say.

'I agree it is a good idea,' he went on, 'but who is going to hang the bell round the cat's neck?'

For a moment there was absolute silence. Then there was an outbreak of coughing and shuffling about.

'Oh, I must go and see to my family.'

'Excuse me, I have to go and remake my nest.'

One of the first of the mice to sneak away was the important one who had the great idea.

PRAYER

Let us think this morning about a well-known phrase: 'Actions speak louder than words'. Help us to remember that it is much more admirable to do important things rather than tell everybody what we are going to do or have done.

HYMN

'One more step' No 47 *The Complete Come and Praise*

Information for the teacher

1. Some further work on 'actions speak louder than words' could be a follow-up from this assembly. Two thought-provoking quotations in this context might be:
   'The time for silence and the time for talk' (Ecclesiastes 3:7).
   'So it is with the tongue: small as it is, it can boast about great things' (James 3:5).

2. Cats rarely feature in symbolic animal stories as creatures with commendable qualities. There is, however, an old legend which claims that, at the birth of Jesus, there was also a cat in the stable which gave birth to a litter of kittens at the same time.

---

60 THE NEWCOMER

Sometimes the way animals behave has a message for how we should behave ourselves. This morning's story gives us an example.

STORY

Jacko was a big, brown, friendly dog. He lived with his owners in a warm, comfortable house. Every day one of them took him for a long walk and he was never kept waiting for food or a long cool drink.

'This is the life,' Jacko used to say to himself and then one day, it happened.

'Here we are.'

Jacko heard his mistress's voice. It sounded odd. Then she came into the room where his basket was. In her arms was a small, black, furry bundle. Jacko couldn't believe his eyes – it was a puppy!

'Come and meet Jacko,' his mistress purred. 'Jacko, this is Oscar. He has come to live with us.'

Jacko growled. How dare they? Why did they want another dog? Wasn't he good enough for them? Jacko put his head on his paws and sulked.

Then his master came in carrying another basket. Carefully he put a soft blanket in it. Then his mistress laid 'it' in the basket.

'He needs a good home, Jacko,' she said, ' and I'm sure you'll look after him.'

For the next few days, Jacko became more and more impatient. Whenever he settled down for a sleep, Oscar climbed into his basket with him. Then he nibbled Jacko's ears, or licked his nose, or pulled his tail – the cheek of it! When they went for a walk, Jacko and their master had to wait while Oscar's pathetic little legs tried to catch up with them.

'What have I done to deserve this?' Jacko moaned to himself.

Then, one bleak winter's morning, Jacko felt awful when he woke up. He couldn't keep warm and shivered all the time. If he got out of his basket, he almost fell over he was so weak. The next few days were dreadful.

The master took him to something called 'the vet's' and he had horrible pills to take. He even had a needle stuck in him! And all the time he felt so weak.

It was funny though that while all this was going on, Oscar seemed to be dreadfully worried about him. He licked Jacko's face, brought him his rubber bone to see if he wanted to play with it and pulled the blankets more cosily round Jacko with his teeth.

Then, after nearly a week, Jacko began to feel better. He got out of his basket one morning and took a deep breath.

'I'm all right,' he thought to himself. 'My legs are strong again. I'm all right!'

As he stood there stretching, Oscar scurried round him, wagging his tail and barking excitedly. Jacko had never seen a dog look so pleased.

'You know,' said Jacko – again to himself because he certainly wouldn't say it aloud yet – 'you're OK Oscar. I reckon we can have real fun together.'

With that he jumped on Oscar and began to nuzzle him with his long nose. Oscar barked even more delightedly.

Then their owners came in.

'Jacko's better!' cried the mistress.

'I'll take them both for a short walk,' replied their master. 'The fresh air will do him good.'

Jacko gave Oscar another nuzzle. Life was good.

PRAYER

Let us pray this morning that we can always avoid selfishness in thought, word and deed. Let us give thanks for brothers, sisters, friends and pets who make our lives more fulfilling, enjoyable and interesting.

HYMN

'Fill your hearts with joy and gladness' No 9 *The Complete Come and Praise*

Information for the teacher

1. Dogs are symbols of watchfulness and fidelity in Christian art. Tobias and Roch are two saints who are particularly associated with faithful dogs.

2. One of the most romantic of dog stories is that of Rin Tin Tin. Found abandoned in a front line trench in the First World War, he was eventually taken to Hollywood where he became a world famous film star, appearing in fifty films.

SPECIAL OCCASIONS

61 THE BADGE OF A GOOD DEED

INTRODUCTION

Soldiers who do brave deeds are given medals. When they wear these everybody recognises that they have done something special. This morning's story is about a bird who looks special for the same reason.

STORY

Hank and his young son Billy were tired, desperately tired. The bitter wind of the Arctic howled round them as they fought their way through the thick snow back to their little wooden hut.

'Christmas Day tomorrow,' sighed Billy to himself. 'At least we have enough food and fuel for that.'

The boy looked up and then said aloud, 'Won't we my friend?'

The little brown bird that flapped around his shoulder gave an answering chirp. It had become a real friend in the cold working days of the winter.

'Nearly home, son,' growled Hank, slapping his son on the back.

Ahead of them was their hut, deeply covered with snow and with icicles hanging from the roof. It would be great to get inside for some warmth and food.

'It certainly will, Dad. But . . . look!'

Billy's voice rose in alarm. The door of the hut had been wrenched off and the snow was drifting inside. Forcing their weary legs to go faster, father and son hurried to their home.

Bursting through the broken door, they gazed around in despair. Their precious fire was almost out, food was damaged and thrown about the room, and the furniture was broken. The whole place looked as if it had been hit by a whirlwind.

'A polar bear – that's who did this,' muttered Hank grimly. 'What's more, he'll be back for us.'

'What shall we do, Dad?' asked a worried Billy.

'Well, first of all, we've got to make the place secure. Doors and windows have to be secured or else the cold will kill us.'

So the two them, already exhausted, set to work. They fixed the door and the windows and set the little cabin to rights as best they could. All the while, the fire, which was already nearly out, got lower and lower.

'Right,' said Hank finally, 'that should do it.'

'Gosh I'm tired, Dad,' replied Billy.

'Me too, son. Tell you what, we'll have a couple of minutes rest and then we'll get that fire going properly.'

So the two of them slumped on the floor. But they were so tired that in less than one minute, they were in a deep sleep.

The little brown bird looked at them and fluttered worriedly round the cabin.

'Wake up, wake up,' it tried to chirp. 'The fire's going out and if it does you'll freeze to death as the temperature plunges down . . . and then there's the bear . . .'

The only answer was the snoring of Hank and Billy.

'What can I do? I must do something,' thought the desperate little bird.

Then the idea came to him. Flying over the dying fire, he got as near to it as he could. Then he started to flap his wings as hard and as often as he possibly could. For what seemed like hours, nothing happened, and then the draught from his flapping wings began to stir the embers of the fire. Soon flames started to appear again but the tired little bird didn't stop. Flap, flap, flap – just millimetres from the fire and then . . .

'Dad, Dad, wake up! The fire! The fire!'

Billy had awakened. After roughly shaking his father awake, the two of them were soon vigorously building the fire up. When they had finished, Billy took the little bird tenderly in his hand. Then he saw that the brown breast was now burned a bright red.

'You poor fellow,' muttered Billy. 'You save our lives and look what it has done to you. From now on I'm going to call you Robin Redbreast.'

And now you know why all robins have red breasts.

PRAYER
Let us think this morning of feeling warm and loved at Christmas. Let us think of families all over the world for whom this is a very special time. Let us pray that peace, calm and safety allow all to enjoy it as they should.

HYMN
'Mary had a baby' No 123 *The Complete Come and Praise*

Information for the teacher
This is an adaptation of a Canadian version of a very well-known story. In its most popular guise, the robin fans the flames of the dying fire in the stable on the night Jesus was born.

---

62   PAPA JACOB'S DOLL'S HOUSE

INTRODUCTION

Sometimes a Christmas present is extra special, as this morning's story shows.

STORY

It was snowing. Icicles stretched down from the roof of the little cottage and a bitter wind swayed the trees round it. Inside the cottage a log fire crackled warmly and there was the sound of singing.

'A tap here . . . a tap-tap there . . . everywhere a tappity-tap.'

The man who was singing was small with a great tangle of wild white hair. He had eyes as green as any Christmas tree and his clothes were very unusual. On one foot he had a blue slipper and on the other a red slipper. His trousers were held up by a knotted black and white scarf and his white shirt was covered in sawdust.

'A tap here . . . a tap-tap there . . . everywhere a tappity-tap-tap.'

As he sang, the man busied himself with tools and pieces of wood. He was making something on the huge table in front of him. It was a doll's house. But not just any doll's house. This was the most magnificent doll's house you have ever seen. It was special; it was for a princess!

'A tap here . . . a tap there . . . everywhere a tappity-tap-tap.'

Nobody who lived in the woods would have been surprised that this was such a beautiful doll's house. They all knew the old man, whose name was Papa Jacob, was the best wood carver for miles around. Now he had heard that a princess had been born in the palace. So he had decided that he would make her the best doll's house he'd ever made and take it to the palace for Christmas.

'Nearly finished,' he hummed to himself. 'It's the day before Christmas Eve. Tomorrow I'll load up the doll's house on my cart and take it to the palace for the princess. A tap-tap here . . . a tap-tap . . .'

Then, above the sound of his singing Papa Jacob heard another tapping. Someone was knocking on his cottage door.

'Come in! The door's open,' shouted the old man cheerily.

He heard no sound.

'Come in,' he shouted again.

Still nothing happened.

Putting down his chisel, Papa Jacob went to the door. He opened it slowly and then gasped. Standing on the door step was a little girl. Despite the bitter cold, she had no coat on and her dress was old and torn. Her thin shoes were soaked through and her straggly hair was wet with snow. She shivered.

'Come in, come in at once, my dear,' said Papa Jacob.

'Please sir, could you spare me some food?' the little girl asked in a tiny voice.

'Of course, come and sit by the fire and I'll get you something that will warm you up.'

When Papa Jacob came back with some hot soup the little girl was still standing up. She was staring at the doll's house with wonder in her eyes.

'It's . . . it's beautiful,' she gasped. 'I've never seen anything so lovely.'

Papa Jacob looked at the house on the table with all the rooms so carefully laid out and the tiny carved figures which looked like real people.

'I'm glad you like it,' he said. 'It's for a real princess.'

'It's so lovely,' whispered the girl.

Now Papa Jacob made her a hot drink on his fire while she ate the soup. When she had finished both, he went into his bedroom and came back with an old jacket. Taking a pair of scissors, he quickly cut the sleeves shorter and then slipped it onto the little girl.

'What's your name?' he asked as he helped her into the coat.

'Maria.'

'Well, I hope this will keep you warmer, Maria. Good luck.'

With a last longing look at the doll's house and a whispered 'thank you' the little girl went out again into the bitter cold.

Papa Jacob got back to putting the finishing touches on the doll's house.

Next morning he was up bright and early. It was Christmas Eve and he had a long way to go. Very, very carefully he loaded the doll's house onto his cart. Then he wrapped lots of sacks round it and tied it down. When this was done he harnessed Old Ben, his horse, to the cart and set off through the carpet of snow.

For more than an hour, they travelled slowly through the wood. Then they arrived at the road which led to the palace. As they did so, many handsome horses pulling fine carriages galloped past them. Papa Jacob saw rich people inside the carriages. They all seemed to be holding beautifully wrapped presents for the princess.

'I haven't seen any doll's houses yet though,' smiled the old man to himself.

Then he reached the palace gates. Still other carriages swept past him through the open gates.

But when Papa Jacob reached the entrance, a soldier stepped out and barred his way.

'What do you want?' he demanded roughly.

'I've brought a present for the princess,' answered the wood carver.

'We've no time for the likes of you and your presents here,' went on the soldier. 'Look out!'

As he shouted the warning, another fine carriage thundered past.

'But it is a doll's house. It has been specially made for . . . .'

'Didn't you hear what I said?' went on the soldier. 'Now come on, get out of the way and don't bother me any more.'

Papa Jacob began to turn his cart round.

'Perhaps if I can find another entrance, round the back maybe, then they'll let me in. I must give the princess her doll's house.'

But as the old man was turning his cart round, another carriage came racing up. Quickly he pulled Ben out of the way but the passing carriage hit the cart and the carefully wrapped doll's house slid off and crashed onto the road. Before Papa Jacob could get to it another carriage smashed straight over it. The precious doll's house was crushed to pieces.

Slowly the old man knelt down and looked at the wreckage. There was no hope of it being repaired. All that remained in one piece was the beautifully carved figure of the princess. He picked it up sadly and began to lead Ben and the cart back home.

It was a long and lonely journey. A tear trickled down Papa Jacob's face and froze in the icy wind as his cottage came in sight. Then, as he got nearer, he saw an old bundle of rags lying on the doorstep.

'I wonder who could have left that there?' he thought. 'But it's not a . . .'

Suddenly the sadness and disappointments of the day vanished from the old man's mind. Leaving Ben, he rushed to his doorstep and swept his old jacket into his arms. Inside it, Maria's body felt like ice.

Pushing the door open with his knee, Papa Jacob laid Maria down beside the fireplace. Running into the bedroom he dragged blankets from his bed. Wrapping her in these, he then set about building the biggest warmest fire he could.

As soon as he had done this, he made Maria a hot drink. Then, whilst he was waiting for the frozen little girl to wake up, he remembered the tiny carved figure of the princess which he still had in his pocket. Taking it out, he stood it beside the drink.

As he did so, Maria's eyes opened.

'What happened?' she whispered.

'You fell asleep, that's all,' replied Papa Jacob kindly. 'Drink this and you'll soon feel better.'

But Maria's eyes were fixed on the carved figure of the princess.

'Can I hold it, please?'

'Of course. It's yours.'

'But the beautiful house – where is it?'

'It's not made yet,' smiled the old man. 'Now you're warm and awake I can get started.'

And as Maria lay beside the blazing fire, Papa Jacob got out his tools and pieces of wood. The last thing she heard as she dozed once more was the sound of the old man singing.

'A tap-tap here . . . a tap-tap there . . . everywhere a tap-tap.'

PRAYER

Let us think of special gifts at Christmas. Gifts of love, kindness, consideration, help and friendliness. Let us pray particularly for those people who are really in need of these special gifts at this time of the year.

HYMN

'Candle in the window (When the winter day is dying)' No 118 *The Complete Come and Praise*

Information for the teacher

Charles Dickens' words on the season are often used but never lose their poignancy:

'There seems a magic in the very name of Christmas. Petty jealousies and discords are forgotten – would that Christmas lasted the whole year through'.

63 A MYSTERY STORY

INTRODUCTION

Christmas is a wonderful time for many people. For others who are lonely or ill, it is less so. This morning's story is a strange one and reminds us that there are many things in the world which remain a mystery to us.

STORY

Emma struggled to get her breath. She lay in bed panting and gasping. She was very ill with pneumonia.

'Oh if only I had somebody to help me,' she whispered to herself.

But she hadn't. She was an old woman and her only daughter had died six months ago. She was alone.

'I'm sure Dr Murray would help me if he knew I was ill,' thought the old woman. 'But I can't even get out of bed.'

Outside Emma's house, the atmosphere was very different. Although a cold wind cut through the streets, there was a feeling of excitement about in the town. After all, it was nearly Christmas; trees sparkled in windows and rosy-cheeked children threw snowballs and went carol-singing.

About a mile away from Emma's house there was a street of tall Victorian houses. In the second of these, lived Dr Murray. For many years, Emma had been his house-keeper.

'Ah well, two days to Christmas,' thought Dr Murray as he sat in an armchair and looked at the flames leaping up from his blazing log fire. 'And time for me to go to bed, I've had a busy day.'

But no sooner had the doctor thought this than there was knocking on his front door.

Dr Murray went to the door and when he opened it he saw the shadowy figure of a woman standing there.

'Doctor,' said the woman, 'I've come to tell you that Emma, your old house-keeper is very ill. If you don't go to see her immediately, she will die before Christmas.'

'Why that's dreadful. Come in a minute, my dear, and I'll get my coat and bag and come to Emma's with you.'

The doctor turned away from the open door and the moaning wind expecting the woman to follow him. But as he reached for his coat, he glanced behind him and she had disappeared.

'How strange,' he thought. 'But perhaps she is so worried that she has hurried back to Emma's ahead of me.'

Pulling his coat and scarf tightly round him and picking up his bag, the doctor stepped out into the winter's night and hurried across town. Half an hour later, he was patting Emma's hand.

'Now,' he said soothingly, 'with more of this medicine and plenty of rest and warmth, you'll be better in no time.'

'Thank you so much, doctor,' said the frail old lady gratefully, 'but who told you I was ill?'

'Your daughter, of course. She came to my house.'

There was a long pause.

'My daughter died six months ago, doctor. Nobody in this world knew I was ill.'

For a long while Dr Murray looked at his patient. When he spoke again it was in a very quiet voice.

'Well I know where several of your friends live. I'll let them know the situation.'

And so, once Emma's friends found out about her, they were all glad to help. She made a complete recovery and by the spring was well again.

But who was the mystery messenger?

PRAYER

Let us pray this morning for those people who are lonely or ill at Christmas. We pray that they may be shown kindness and given hope. Amen.

HYMN

'Standing in the rain' No 125 *The Complete Come and Praise*

Information for the teacher

1. There are several tales of Christmas which have an element of mystery in them. One of the most famous is that of Baboushka. The three kings call at her cottage to rest on their way to see the Christ Child. They invite the old Russian woman to join them on their journey. She delays to clean her cottage and sadly when she follows them later she can no longer see the guiding star. For weeks she seeks the way to Bethlehem. Finally she gets there, long after everyone has left the stable. But she puts her humble present of black bread on the empty crib and lies down to sleep. Next day she is found dead there. Children in Russia still get a piece of black bread with their presents as a reminder of the legend.

2. As an alternative to the prayer suggested a few words from the 'Cherry Tree Carol' might be used: 'As Joseph was a-walking he heard an angel sing, This night shall be the birth, of Christ the heavenly King'.

3. The following poem also offers another alternative:

Then

A little town,
Shaded by hills and olive groves
Waited
For five days.

In this time
Through weary hours and bitter nights
Journeyed
The young couple.

'I'm worried,'
Said the husband to his patient wife.
'Will there
Be room for us?'

Crowded streets,
Buyers, traders, soldiers, goats,
Nowhere
To seek rest.

'Best I've got,'
The harassed landlord said at last,
'But it's
Only a stable.'

And so that night,
Manger cradled in soft, clean straw,
Was born
The world's Saviour.

---

64 THE FIRST CHRISTMAS TREE

INTRODUCTION
One of the delights of Christmas is to look around and see beautifully lit Christmas trees everywhere. This morning's story is about a very brave man and, perhaps, the first Christmas tree.

STORY
'You're a very brave man,' said the Pope to the monk who stood in front of him.

'I don't know if I'm that brave though,' replied the monk, whose name was Wynfrith.

'Don't underestimate your courage, my son,' continued the Pope calmly. 'You wouldn't be known to everybody as Boniface unless you deserved the nickname.'

Boniface smiled. Nobody called him Wynfrith anymore. It was always Boniface, which meant 'doer of good'.

The two men were in Rome in 710 AD. Boniface had been walking through Europe preaching Christianity. Now he was about to go to Germany, but there savage pagan tribes were as likely to kill Christian missionaries as listen to them.

And so, some weeks later, Boniface and a friend were walking through a deep forest near the German village of Geismar, near the river Rhine. It was late December and a bleak, bitterly cold night.

'Look, there's torchlight ahead,' muttered Boniface's friend, pointing to flickering shining through the dark trees.

'I don't like the look of that,' replied Boniface, stroking his chin anxiously.

Both men had heard of terrible human sacrifices which took place in this area. Children were often killed to please the great pagan god Thor. These dreadful deeds took place underneath a huge oak tree which the pagan Germans thought was sacred.

Nervously the two men pressed on. Then they were in a clearing and a terrifying sight was lit by a ring of blazing torches.

Underneath an enormous oak tree, a small boy, tightly bound with rope, lay whimpering piteously. All around were brutal-looking heavily-armed men. One of them was just beginning to raise an axe when . . .

Taking in the terrible scene at a glance, Boniface's nervousness vanished instantly. Striding across the clearing, he seized the axe from the gigantic German and, turning, he began to chop ruthlessly at the oak tree.

As each blow cracked into the tree, something strange began to happen. Just as a cry of rage started to boil up from the tribesmen, a violent wind whistled and thrashed through the trees. At each stroke of Boniface's axe, the oak began to bend more and more as the wind roared round it.

Then, as the crowd watched in fear, there was a tremendous crack! Scattering quickly, the pagans flung themselves aside as the tree crashed down in the clearing.

For a minute there was frozen silence. The bound boy, the dozens of pagans and the two monks all seemed rooted where they stood.

Then Boniface saw another amazing sight and acted quickly. There between the roots of the fallen oak was a shoot only a few inches high. It was a tiny, evergreen spruce tree.

Seizing a nearby torch, Boniface held it over the little evergreen.

'Look,' he called to the crowd. 'Here is a sign of the good news I bring you. This beautiful young tree will remind you that this is the night your great oak fell and a new tree told you of the coming of Jesus Christ.'

And so, in that German wood all those years ago, a brave man first used the symbol of the Christmas tree to pass on his wonderful news.

PRAYER
Let us think this morning about the wonder of Christmas and the joy it brings to so many people. Let us give thanks for the sight of so many

Christmas trees which are decorated with thought and care. Let us remember the message of the first Christmas.

HYMN
'The holly and the ivy' No 119 *The Complete Come and Praise*

Information for the teacher
1. St Boniface (christened Wynfrith) was born in Crediton, England in 675 AD and died in Germany in 754. He left England in 718 to preach Christianity in Germany. He is now best remembered in the latter country and his tomb at Fulda is considered a very sacred area.

2. The significance of the Christmas tree in the UK also owes much to Germany. It was Queen Victoria's husband, Prince Albert, who introduced and popularised the German custom of decorating a fir-tree here. Nobody created better images of Victorian Christmases than Charles Dickens: 'Up flew the bright sparks in myriads as the logs were stirred. The deep red blaze sent forth a rich glow that penetrated into the furthest corner of the room and cast its cheerful tint on every face.'

---

65 CHRISTMAS IS A TIME FOR PEACE

INTRODUCTION
At Christmas in 1914, Britain and Germany were at war with each other. Despite their orders to fight however, ordinary British and German soldiers put down their weapons and joined each other in singing carols on Christmas Day. The generals were furious about this and said it must never happen again. Most people know now what happened in 1914 but fewer people know what happened in 1915.

STORY
It was Christmas Eve in 1915. In France, British and German soldiers sat in trenches just a hundred metres apart. For the whole of the past year they had been firing guns and trying to kill each other.

Then, in the crisp night air of that long-ago Christmas Eve, a lovely sound came from the German trenches. It was the sound of hundreds of men singing a carol together. The British soldiers listened quietly and, when the carol was finished, they started to sing too.

As the moon bathed the desolate scene, one carol after another was sung. Then voices began to shout from each of the trenches.

'Merry Christmas' shouted the British soldiers to the Germans.

'Merry Christmas' called back the Germans.

Next, lights began to appear and, from the German trenches, soldiers started to clamber out. Seeing them, the British soldiers lit lamps too and went out to meet their so-called enemies. Soon the no-man's land between the trenches was full of soldiers from both sides. They shook hands with each other and exchanged little presents of sweets and cigarettes. It did not seem to matter that not many of the soldiers could speak the other's language.

Afterwards many soldiers wrote down what they felt about this wonderful, yet sad, occasion.

'There wouldn't have been a war if it had been left to ordinary people.'

'We had a great time with our enemies and parted with much hand-shaking and mutual goodwill.'

'It didn't seem right to be killing each other at Christmas time.'

What is so sad is that so many of these men were later killed in this dreadful war. The war went on until November 1918 but there are no records of further truces in 1916 or 1917.

PRAYER
Let us pray this Christmas for peace everywhere. Peace where families are gathered together; peace where life is hard or dangerous; and peace where people are finding it difficult to live together.

HYMN
'Christmas time' No 127 *The Complete Come and Praise*

Information for the teacher
1. Very little information exists about this second truce on the Western Front. There is plenty of scope for extending this theme in the modern world and it also lends itself as introductory material for themes like responsibility, hardship, courage, comradeship, etc.

2. As an alternative to the prayer given, the words of a prayer attributed to St Francis of Assisi could be used:
Lord make me an instrument of your peace.
Where there is hatred let me sow love,
Where there is injury, pardon,
Where there is doubt, faith,
Where there is despair, hope,
Where there is darkness, light,
Where there is sadness, joy.

66 EASTER

INTRODUCTION
First of all this morning let us think about beginnings.

STORY
Those of you who have younger brothers and sisters will know that one of the most exciting beginnings in a family is when a new baby is born. As with all good beginnings, a great deal of preparation is involved.

You will know that your parents bought baby clothes ready for the new arrival, picked a cot for them and chose a place for it in the bedroom. Then there's the pushchair and all the talk about what the baby is going to be called.

Easter is a time for new beginnings too and Christians prepare for it just as thoroughly.

For instance, let us think about the number forty. If you are a mathematician, you might think that forty means eight times five, or four times ten or two times twenty. But if you are a Christian, you know that forty is an important number because before Easter there is the season of Lent and it is forty days long.

During this time, Christians think especially about the first Easter and the time leading up to it. They feel that this might help them to be more understanding and better people. To help them concentrate their minds on this, they often give up something they really like during Lent, such as chocolate or their favourite food.

Then after Good Friday comes Easter Sunday. This is when all Christians think about new life and a joyful service is held in church when the great Easter candle is lit.

One of the greatest of all Christian churches in England is Durham Cathedral and the story of its beginning is a very unusual one. Long ago, a band of monks were making their way through the countryside in northern England. They had with them the coffin of a famous monk called Cuthbert. He had told the others before he died that they should carry his coffin and wait for a message which would tell them where to bury him.

'Come on, come on,' cried the monk who was leading the horse. The horse was pulling the cart which carried Cuthbert's coffin. That is to say he had been pulling the cart but had suddenly stopped for no reason at all.

'What's the matter?' asked another of the monks.

'I don't know. He just won't go on.'

As it was nearly dark, the monks decided to stop where they were and camp there. The next morning one of them woke up with a start.

'I've just had an amazing dream,' he said. 'God wants us to bury Cuthbert at Durham.'

'But where is that?' queried another.

None of them knew.

'Well,' continued the monk, 'I think it must be near here and that's why the horse stopped so suddenly.'

Just at that moment an angry-looking woman approached them.

'Excuse me,' said one of the monks, 'but do you know where Durham is?'

'That's a strange question,' replied the woman. 'I've lost my cow and I'm sure she's wandered off in that direction. Follow me and I'll show you.'

So they all went off together and in no time at all they found the cow. She was munching grass on a bank which towered over a quietly meandering river.

'This beautiful spot must be the place,' muttered one of the monks.

So they knelt in prayer and then buried Cuthbert on that lovely spot. Later they built a simple church there. And from this beginning the church was eventually rebuilt as the huge and magnificent cathedral which now stands high above the River Wear at Durham.

PRAYER

Dear God, Help us to remember that beginnings are important through our lives. Please give us energy and enthusiasm as we begin each new day. Help us to find joy as we travel through it and strength to cope with any disappointments it might hold. Help us to feel and celebrate the joy of Easter Day. Amen.

HYMN

'Now the green blade rises' No 131 *The Complete Come and Praise*

Information for the teacher

1. Easter is a difficult concept for primary children but it does highlight several themes which are fruitful to follow. Apart from beginnings these could include: hope, families, traditions and awe.

2. The old folk-tale of Cuthbert's burial ground is linked to the fact that in 875 the monks of Lindisfarne, off the Northumbrian coast, sought a resting place for his body. The first Norman bishop, William, started the cathedral in 1093. It was fully completed in 1499 after centuries of building.

---

67 HERE IS THE PLACE

INTRODUCTION
Muslims call their holy buildings mosques. They also believe that the whole of the world is a mosque and that they can pray anywhere. But how was it decided where the first ever mosque would be? That is an interesting story.

STORY
The journey had been long, hot and dusty and the travellers were very tired.

'Well,' said Hassan, peering ahead from his camel, 'there's Medina in front of us.'

'You're right,' agreed Husseyn, whose camel was loping alongside. 'Now our master might be able to do his work properly.'

Their leader, along with many of his followers, rode behind. He was Muhammad. He was trying to get people to believe in God and was looking for a place where they could settle. And there, in the scorching hot land ahead, Medina stood before them beneath the setting sun.

Once Muhammad and the Muslims had settled down in the town, another problem arose.

'We need to build somewhere where we can all meet.'

'It needs to be big.'

'It has to be on an important spot.'

This was the sort of thing that was being said. Many of his followers were very keen to please Muhammad. They came to him one after the other.

'Master, I have two really big houses. I would be very pleased to give you one of them.'

'We need our building on a suitable piece of land. I own the perfect spot. I'll be glad to give it to you.'

'Master, please take my house and my land.'

Muhammad listened to them all. Then he gathered everybody together and spoke.

'My friends, thank you for all your offerings. But we must remember that we can pray anywhere. All we want is a large, convenient building where we can all meet. Now we are going to choose a piece of land and get on with making our mosque.'

'But,' asked someone, 'just how are we going to choose?'

'Are you going to make the choice?' asked another.

The wise Muhammad smiled and then he beckoned Hassan to come to him.

'Hassan, my friend, please bring my camel here.'

Everybody knew how Muhammad loved his camel but why did he need it now?

Scuffing the dust, the camel was led to the leader. Muhammad stroked its head and untied its tether. Now free, the camel began to wander around. Muhammad followed it and so did everybody else.

Eventually, right in the middle of a scruffy piece of wasteland, the camel became tired. Slowly it bent its great long legs and sat down.

'There,' said Muhammad. 'We'll build our first mosque right there.'

PRAYER

Let us pray. Let us remember in our prayers this morning that there need not be a special place to have good thoughts. We can think them any time in any place.

HYMN

'Let the world rejoice together' No 148 *The Complete Come and Praise*

Information for the teacher

1. Muhammad was a seventh century Arabian trader when he was visited by an angel in a cave near Hira. This was in 610.

2. There are obviously several Muslim festivals this story could be linked to but Id-ul-Fitr is one recommendation because it is so enjoyed by children. This celebrates the end of the month of fasting called Ramadan (November/December in Western calendars) and features the sighting of the new moon, special foods, new clothes and presents. Cards are sent wishing their recipients 'Id Mubarak', which means 'Happy Festival'.

3. Giving is so often a feature of all religions and there is a particularly useful Muslim quotation in this context: 'You will never attain righteousness until you give freely of what you love' (*Qur'an*).

68 THE LAMP

INTRODUCTION

Why are some people outstanding footballers or musicians? Why are some people very brave and others not? 'Why' – we can use this word often because there are many mysteries in the world. Here is the story of one of them.

STORY

Ruth and Naomi were excited. They lived hundreds and hundreds of years ago and something very special had just happened.

'I heard Father say that they were going to light the lamp in the temple today,' said Ruth.

'That's right,' replied Naomi, 'everything is ready in the temple again. Isn't it marvellous?'

There had been a great battle and Judah Maccabee had driven away the Greeks. Now Ruth and Naomi, like all Jews, could worship in the temple again.

Later the same day, they went to the temple with their father. There was a huge crowd there. Everybody was happy to be free again but a whisper started to go round and faces became worried.

'What is it?' whispered Naomi, after the man next to them muttered in their father's ear.

'There's a problem with the temple light.'

'Oh.'

Naomi and Ruth knew that the temple lamp was very important. It must never ever be allowed to go out.

'Yes,' continued their father, 'it has been lit as you can see, but there is only enough oil to keep it alight for today and it will take eight days to prepare a fresh supply of oil.'

'That means . . .' began Ruth.

'It will die and stay out for all that time,' said Naomi, completing the sentence.

All around them were worried faces. How could things go wrong again so quickly?

That night, when the girls went home, they talked for ages about this.

'Tomorrow we must go and see if the lamp is still alight,' said Ruth.

And so they went to the temple early in the morning and went in very quietly. Others were there and the lamp was still burning.

For day after day, the two girls did the same thing and the mystery continued. The lamp which had oil for only one day kept burning and burning. Finally one afternoon their father came in with a very contented look on his face.

'The oil,' he said. 'It is now prepared and we don't need to worry any more.'

'Eight days,' gasped Ruth.

'That's right,' added Naomi. 'That's how long the lamp stayed alight with only one day's oil in it.'

'Yes,' said their father, 'there are many things we don't understand in this life but that is a miracle.'

PRAYER

Let us pray this morning for a miracle that there is peace everywhere in the world. Let there be a time when no one hurts their neighbour and no one wants what belongs to someone else.

HYMN

'Shalom' No 141 *The Complete Come and Praise*

Information for the teacher

1. This story relates directly to the events remembered at the Jewish festival of Hanukkah. This takes place in the Jewish months of Kislev and Tevet (December in Western calendars). It can be linked with Diwali and Christmas as a 'festival of light'.

2. Every synagogue has a perpetual lamp in it. This is in front of the Ark which contains the Scrolls. These are made of parchment and the *Torah* is written on them.

3. In connection with the prayer contemplating peace, there is an evocative biblical quotation which might be used with older children:
   'Wolves and sheep will live together in peace,
   and leopards will lie down with young goats.
   Calves and lion cubs will feed together,
   and little children will take care of them'
   (Isaiah 11: 6).

69 THE KNIGHT'S STORY

INTRODUCTION

When somebody does something really horrible to us it is not easy to forgive them. Think about this for a moment and then listen carefully to the poem which begins our assembly.

STORY

'The mountain is the mountain
And the way is the same as of old.
What has changed
Is my own heart.'

Now we can ask ourselves, 'What does this mean?'

That is not an easy question to answer but if we listen to the story which tells us how the poem came to be written then we have a much better understanding of it.

Many, many years ago there was a Japanese knight who came to believe in a religion called Buddhism. This meant that he had to give up all fighting and he decided to become a monk.

He did this and went to live in a monastery with many other monks. There they prayed, worked hard and tried to do as much good as they could.

After many years, our monk had to make a journey. Now, on this journey, he happened to meet a knight coming towards him. The two men got nearer and then passed each other. No sooner had they done so than the knight turned and called back to the monk.

'Stop! Stay there!'

The monk stopped.

The knight came back and looked again at the monk.

'I thought it was . . . yes . . . I know you.'

When the monk looked carefully, he saw that this was a knight he had known many years ago when he was a knight himself. What was more, this man had been an enemy. He remembered the challenges and the fighting.

The knight spoke again.

'I said I know you.'

This time he spoke very threateningly indeed.

The monk didn't answer and this seemed to enrage the knight even more. He obviously wanted to fight and, to challenge the monk, he spat in his face.

For a moment, the monk felt all the old urges of his life of so many years ago. Then he thought of his time praying in the monastery and what he had learned there.

Calmly he took out a piece of cloth and wiped the spittle from his face. Then he walked quietly on and, when he eventually he got back to the monastery, he wrote the poem with which we started this assembly.

PRAYER

Let us pray this morning about the way we behave. We all do things we shouldn't do at times and it is then that we hope people will forgive us. Let us think carefully about the following words: to err is human, to forgive is divine.

HYMN

'The pollen of peace (O let us spread the pollen of peace)' No 145 *The Complete Come and Praise*

Information for the teacher

1. All Buddhists hope ultimately to reach nirvana (a state of complete happiness and peace). One of the steps on the Eightfold Path in seeking to achieve this is to think the right thoughts, which means letting go of personal wants and desires, acting with kindness and avoiding hurting anything.

2. One of the festivals at which this assembly might be used is Wesak which is the combined celebration of the Buddha's birth, his enlightenment and his ultimate reaching of nirvana. Lighting lanterns is a feature of the celebrations while other aspects of it which children enjoy are street stalls and theatres.

3. There is a useful quotation in 'The Songs of Milarepa': 'Everything I see and hear is a teacher'.

---

70 SAVED BY A BIRD

INTRODUCTION

When we think of a peacock, we think of the beautiful colours in its tail. But this was not always the case. Once, the peacock's feathers were a dull brown and nobody would give him a second glance. How did the feathers change colour? Listen and you will find out.

STORY

'Boring,' said the peacock to himself as he scratched about on the hard ground.

'It is so boring standing here scratching for insects.'

He looked bored too. His dull brown feathers hung limply as his harsh, ugly feet raked the earth.

Then, suddenly, he was aware of another sound. Someone was running fast and in a panic. The peacock looked up. To his astonishment he saw that it was Indra. But Indra was a god – what could he possibly be running away from?

'Who is chasing you?' gasped the amazed peacock.

'Ravana!' was the anguished reply.

The peacock understood at once. Ravana was the demon king whose powers were even greater than the sky god Indra's.

'But nobody can run faster than Ravana,' called out the peacock desperately. 'Quick, I'll hide you.'

He spread out his huge tail and Indra curled up behind it.

This was no sooner done than the demon king appeared. His huge feet pounded the ground in the chase. He ignored the peacock completely and rushed on in the direction which he thought Indra had taken.

Gradually the terrible pounding faded and Indra cautiously emerged from behind the tail. First of all, he looked to see if there was any sign of the demon king returning. When he was sure there was not, he turned back to the peacock.

'Thank you,' he said. 'Without you I would have been lost. For what you have done today you deserve to be the most beautiful bird in the world.'

No sooner had he spoken than the peacock's feathers began to change colour. Slowly the brown began to glisten and then it turned into the most spectacular mixture of blue and green.

'Oh,' gasped the peacock. 'Oh, oh, oh.'

Indra had disappeared by now but the bird continued to stare at his wonderful colours.

'They're . . . they're just marvellous.'

Then, however, he glanced down and saw his feet were still ugly. Quickly he lowered his lovely new tail.

'Wonderful feathers and ugly feet. At least these feet will remind me of what I once looked like all over.'

So the peacock might be beautiful, but he is also brave and can remember when he was very ordinary.

PRAYER

Let us think this morning about being prepared. Being prepared to give help when it is unexpectedly needed. Being prepared to remember that things we are good at are gifts for which we should be thankful. But let us not forget to share, enjoy and celebrate these gifts.

HYMN

'Who put the colours in the rainbow?' No 12 *The Complete Come and Praise*

Information for the teacher

1. This story could be used in conjunction with Diwali. One link is the presence of Ravana. It was the demon king Ravana who kidnapped Sita. Diwali celebrates the return of Rama and Sita after the former, with the help of Hanuman, has killed the demon and rescued Sita.

2. Diwali is celebrated in the Hindu month of Aswin (October/November in Western calendars). Gifts are offered to Lakshmi, the goddess of wealth and good fortune, and lamps are lit everywhere so that she can look into houses. Coloured patterns are spread on the ground to attract her. It is the most widely-celebrated Hindu festival.

Class assemblies

With regard to class assemblies in this book, the same approach has been taken as for the complete assemblies. Each class assembly can be used instantly. There are sections in each which can be photocopied to facilitate this. More than with the complete assemblies, those presented by a class can be enhanced, or limited, by many factors and the class teacher must consider all of these when preparing the following assemblies.

The first limitation is that presentation areas can vary enormously. Halls range from spacious, staged and well lit to long, cramped and aged and they do not exist at all in some very small schools. The second limitation is equipment. Whereas some schools have everything (stages, curtains, staging blocks, spotlights, excellent sound systems, copious musical instruments and taped/recorded music), others have a much smaller range of equipment.

The expertise and interests of the teacher and, often as a result, the pupils in their care need to be considered as well. For example, some classes are particularly talented and experienced in dramatic work, music, choral speech or working with props. Some teachers are also able to enlist valuable outside help from parents, helpers and knowledgeable members of the community, while others have to do virtually everything themselves.

Thus, every class assembly can be moulded by the specific circumstances which apply to the school. However, some requirements are mandatory. Unless the presentation is pre-recorded for amplification to mimed effects, it must be audible at all times. Similarly, the presentation should be arranged so that all the action is always visible to the audience.

Whilst each assembly should have a definite aim and purpose, it should never be boring. It should be stimulating, thought-provoking, varied and never too long! A good class assembly is always looked forward to by the audience of children, teachers, parents, helpers, etc. and it should be a rewarding experience for all concerned.

71 CHOOSING A PATH

AIM: in the widest sense, to 'enhance the children's own spiritual, moral, cultural and social development' and acquire some knowledge of a principal religion' (SCAA, 1999).

MATERIALS REQUIRED: a map of the local area (enlarged if possible) and eight placards, each bearing the word 'RIGHT'. Although not essential, it would be helpful to show a drawing of the eight-spoked wheel symbolising the Buddhist Eightfold Path.

NUMBERS INVOLVED: whole class, with many speakers required for short and long passages.

ENTRY MUSIC: music could be chosen from one of two themes. As the first main feature of the assembly is journeys then travel music would be appropriate. Suggested choices are Eric Coates' *Coronation Scot* and the signature tunes of television programmes such as 'Wish you were here' and 'Holiday'. Alternatively, as the second main feature of the assembly concerns Buddhism, music associated with this would be equally relevant.

SCRIPT: see p 153

72 SPECIAL PEOPLE

AIM: to emphasise the fact that everybody is special.

MATERIALS REQUIRED: books and photographs. In almost every school, there are books about famous and heroic people. Make a collection of these and of some photographs of famous people which could be cut out of newspapers and magazines.

NUMBERS INVOLVED: whole class.

ENTRY MUSIC: fanfare music, such as 'March of the Gladiators', 'Arrival of the Queen of Sheba' and 'When the Saints go Marching in'.

Teacher's note – Biblical reference for the Biblical material in the script is Ecclesiasticus 44: 1–15. Also, the teacher should read the prayer for this assembly.

SCRIPT: see p 156

73 BELONGING TO A COMMUNITY

AIM: to examine the benefits and responsibilities of belonging to a community and to consider some special places.

MATERIALS REQUIRED: pictures or artefacts relating to a church, a mosque and the River Ganges; a small jar of water; and the construction of a 'wall'. It is also useful to have some placards denoting important Islamic words such as 'Minaret', 'Muezzin', 'Allah', 'Mecca', etc.

NUMBERS INVOLVED: whole class, with a variety of speakers.

ENTRY MUSIC: some martial music for audience entry.

Teacher's note: the teacher should read the conclusion of the presentation.

SCRIPT: see p 158

74 COLOUR, COLOUR, COLOUR

AIM: to help us appreciate the vibrancy of different colours in our lives and the significance of colours when associated with different events, cultures and religions.

MATERIALS REQUIRED: pieces of paper, each of a different colour; a wedding ring; a black and white chequered flag; a football shirt; an example of the school uniform; and a pair of cymbals.

NUMBERS INVOLVED: whole class, pre-arranged groups and a team of speakers.

ENTRY MUSIC: a pianist, or tape, plays any music associated with colour as the audience come in. At an appropriate moment this changes to the hymn 'Who put the colours in the rainbow' No 12 *The Complete Come and Praise* and everybody joins in with the singing.

SCRIPT: see p 161

75 SETTING AN EXAMPLE

AIM: to use an inspirational religious leader to show how others can be inspired by outstanding behaviour.

MATERIALS REQUIRED: a copy of the Qur'an and Qur'an stand (in many cases, this will not be possible and simulations can be used); various costumes and props for the drama; and a bowl of water.

NUMBERS INVOLVED: whole class, with some pupils required to speak and act.

ENTRY MUSIC: music with a Middle Eastern theme would be useful. A quiet passage from *Scheherazade* could be used to suggest contemplation or other 'thoughtful' music would be appropriate.

SCRIPT: see p 163

76 STORIES AT CHRISTMAS

AIM: to remind ourselves of words and music which help to make this such a wonderful festival by recalling two stories of Christmas.

MATERIALS REQUIRED: robes for three kings; rags for the little girl; a post disguised as a staff for the Glastonbury enactment; and the stable door to Jesus's birth place. A posy of tissue paper roses would also be useful.

NUMBERS INVOLVED: whole class, divided into groups for acting, singing and reading.

ENTRY MUSIC: a medley of Christmas carols.

SCRIPT: see p 165

77 GOOD TIMES AND BAD

This is preferably a winter assembly.

AIM: to think about disappointments, difficulties and how to overcome them and keeping a balanced point of view.

MATERIALS REQUIRED: pictures, natural specimens and artefacts which remind us of winter, and coats, anoraks, etc.

NUMBERS INVOLVED: whole class, with groups for choral speaking and individual contributions.

ENTRY MUSIC: the music for this assembly should evoke cold or loneliness. A useful alternative here is a compilation of sound effects (such as those available from the BBC) or a tape which the children have made themselves of winter sounds.

SCRIPT: see p 167

78 IT MAKES ME THINK

AIM: to make us realise the importance and significance of words and actions and to increase awareness of some religious activities.

MATERIALS REQUIRED: some red and gold thread; three large cards with the numbers '7', '5' and '3' on them; pictures of fireworks; some cards bearing pleasurably evocative words such as 'chocolate', 'holiday', etc.; and a collection of party noise-makers.

NUMBERS INVOLVED: whole class, with all involved in readings, displaying placards, enacting scenes and blowing party noise-makers.

ENTRY MUSIC: music should be lively and cheerful.

Teacher's note – the teacher introduces the second section of the presentation.

SCRIPT: see p 169

79 FACTS OF A DISASTER

Teacher's note: This is quite a complex assembly at first glance, less so with the visual and dramatic effects. Pupils enjoy presenting it and the message has considerable impact. The assembly is intended for presentation by older primary pupils and is a dramatisation of a story which appeared in Redvers Brandling's *This Morning's Story* (Nash and Pollock, 1996).

AIM: to appreciate the importance of responsibility and rules. The assembly also covers signs and symbols.

MATERIALS REQUIRED: a red flag; a white flag; a 'tunnel' (e.g. a curtained recess in the hall, or something similar which allows the pupils to enter, disappear from view and re-emerge; several placards, some bearing the word 'MISTAKE' and others bearing the word 'RESPONSIBILITY'; and some cymbals and drums.

NUMBERS INVOLVED: whole class, three groups of four children, holding each other's waists to form trains, two flag-wavers and various speakers.

ENTRY MUSIC: some recorded train sounds (such as *Coronation Scot,* 'Chatanooga Choo Choo', etc.) or taped sound effects.

Teacher's note – the teacher summarises the events from the main presentation. Also, to emphasise serious reflection, the pupils could leave the hall in silence.

SCRIPT: see p 171

80 SPECIAL DAYS

AIM: to look at some special days; to help realise that every day of our lives is a special day; and to appreciate the gift of life.

MATERIALS REQUIRED: miners' costumes; a banner depicting aspects of mining; a clock-face showing midnight; some pupils prepared for a passage of country dancing (morris dancing would be ideal); and some lanterns made from coloured materials such as paper, silk, etc.

NUMBERS INVOLVED: whole class and groups to act, display material and provide commentary.

ENTRY MUSIC: some celebration music should be used for presenting class and audience entry. Pieces with a day theme would be ideal, for example 'Morning has broken', 'It's going to be a great day' or 'Some day he'll come along'.

SCRIPT: see p 174

Drama in assembly

Good Morning Everybody began this section with the following quotation. This provides such a telling case for the use of drama in assembly that it is repeated here.

'[Drama] provides an outlet for self-expression and helps the development of imagination and artistic awareness; it increases social awareness, fluency of speech, self-knowledge, self-respect, self-discipline and self-confidence. It gives children the opportunity to learn how to co-operate with others and helps develop orderly thinking and the ability to organise . . . It may also have a therapeutic effect, through helping children to deal with real life problems, or a cathartic effect, by enabling them to act out violence and frustration. It provides social and moral training.' (from *One Hundred Plus Ideas for Drama* by Anna Scher and Charles Verrall. Reprinted by permission of Heinemann Educational Publishers.)

The purpose of this section is to provide the primary teacher with more resources and ideas which they can adapt or extend for drama in assembly. They can be used in various ways for example, with the presenter involving a number of children spontaneously, via mimes with a scripted commentary and via a scripted and well-prepared presentation.

The following sections provide help in all of these areas:

- ideas for drama – a simple list from which the teacher can choose, extend and develop
- dramatic possibilities linked to special occasions – a month by month list containing some religious and secular events and anniversaries
- useful quotations – a list of quotations which could stimulate dramatic ideas
- drama development – mimes and scripted plays.

Ideas for drama

SIMPLE STARTERS

This is simply a list of ideas which have dramatic potential for assembly.

The promise
A friend in need
That was brave
I didn't mean to but . . .
If only . . .
I wish I hadn't said that
Try, try, try again
They're not like us
Be prepared
I didn't have time
I can't be bothered
Please
Thank you
The new boy/girl
Together
A little goes a long way
Behaving stupidly
Making the most of an opportunity
Doing the best you can
Different points of view
Family
To err is human, to forgive is divine
Excuses
Temptation
What's the point of rules?
Sharing
All that glitters
Greed
It's their fault
Joy
The hero/heroine

A lesson learnt from an animal
Loyalty
Honesty
Using gifts given to us
Isn't that lovely?
How can I help?
The good turn
People in need
Tolerance
School is . . .
If I could only have one wish
That is really important!
Why did you do that?
The message
I never expected them to help
My gran says . . .
Everybody's got a story
Help from a letter
I don't know
Are you content? (see Drama development, p 150)
To give is to receive (see Drama development, p 150)
Greed gets nothing (see Drama development, p 150)
The silver lining (see Scripted plays, p 151)
Gifts (see Scripted plays, p 151)
Modesty (see Scripted plays, p 152)

Dramatic possibilities linked to special occasions

Throughout the year, there are many religious and secular occasions and anniversaries which have dramatic potential. Many of these are so well-known that to detail them is unnecessary. The aim in this section, therefore, is to concentrate mainly on some lesser-known occasions which could be dramatised. These are listed below and are arranged by month. The dates of some religious festivals can vary and the dates given below are approximate in these cases (for sources of current religious calendar information, see p 196).

SEPTEMBER

Religious occasions

HARVEST FESTIVAL gathering in the harvest; machines in action; different kinds of harvest – fish, coal, etc. A less predictable approach might be to dramatise the institution of the modern harvest festival. This is attributed to Rev. R. S. Hawker, who became vicar of Morwenstow in Cornwall in 1834 and proposed that people bring seasonal offerings to God.

ROSH HASHANAH Jewish New Year, joyful celebration welcomed by blowing a ram's horn (shofar). On New Year's Eve people eat apples dipped in honey as a symbol of a 'sweet' new year.

SUKKOT Jewish Feast of Tabernacles, celebrated with offerings of grapes, fruits, olives and palms. Children are given sweets, fruit and flags; festivities include dancing.

DASSHERA a Hindu celebration of events in the life of Rama. Mainly Northern India.

1st   Feast day of St Giles. He protected a deer by standing in the way of an arrow fired at it by a hunter and is now regarded as the patron saint of disabled people.

14th   Holy Rood Day – when in the fourth century St Helena found the cross on which it was supposed that Jesus had died.

16th   The Pilgrim Fathers sailed from Plymouth to America on the *Mayflower*.

21st   St Matthew's Day. He gave up tax collecting to be Jesus's disciple.

27th   St Vincent de Paul died in 1660. A very practical saint, he once took the place of a galley slave to show his humanity.

29th   Michaelmas – after St Michael, the protector of those who tried to overcome evil.

Secular occasions

2nd   The Great Fire of London began in 1666.

4th   Pindar, the Greek poet, was born in 518 BC. He said, 'Mirth is the best physician.'

8th   The date on which Abraham Lincoln said, 'You can fool some of the people all of the time, and all of the people some of the time, but you can not fool all of the people all of the time.'

10th   Scapegoat day, a traditional Jewish custom where a goat was let loose in the desert to take away the sins of the people.

12th   The day on which Orville Wright stayed airborne for a new record time of one hour, fourteen minutes and twenty seconds in 1908.

14th   George Frederick Handel finished writing his *Messiah* in 1742 after working for twenty-three days non-stop.

15th   Scottish bacteriologist Alexander Fleming discovered penicillin in 1928.

22nd   Two men and seven women were executed for being witches at Salem, Massachusetts in 1692.

27th   In 1880 electric lights were introduced in London.

OCTOBER

Religious occasions

4th   Feast day of St Francis of Assisi. One dramatic but less well-known story about him is that he heard God say to him, 'Repair my falling house.' Taking this literally he took a bale of goods from his father's warehouse to pay for the repair of St Damiano's church. His father was furious and disowned him. Thus St Francis set off in poverty about his life's work.

8th   Muhammad entered Medina on a camel in 622.
18th   Feast day of St Luke. He was a doctor, painter and writer, as well as being a disciple of Jesus.
25th   In 287 St Crispin was executed for his beliefs by the Emperor Maximian. Crispin preached during the day and made shoes at night. Hence, he is the patron saint of cobblers.

Secular occasions

7th   John Evelyn the diarist visited a slave ship on this date in 1644. He wrote 'hundreds of miserably naked persons . . . double chained about their waists and legs . . . and all commanded by a cruel and imperious seaman.'
12th   Elizabeth Fry, prison reformer died in 1845.
15th   Florence Nightingale began her work in Scutari hospital in the Crimea in 1854.
20th   *The Sunday Times* was first issued in 1822.
22nd   Andre-Jacques Garnerin made the first successful parachute descent in Paris in 1797.

NOVEMBER

Religious occasions

DIWALI Hindu festival of lights celebrated in October or November. Theme of making things brighter – related to the Rama and Sita story. Features lights (lamps and candles); new clothes; presents; music; fireworks; and open-air dancing.

5th   There is a dramatic Old Testament story which could be linked to the bonfires traditionally associated with November 5th.
       'Elijah gathered the Israelites on Mount Carmel and spoke to them. "I am God's prophet," he said, "but there are many who claim to be prophets but who are false. I am going to prove them false."
       So saying Elijah had an ox put on a pile of wood ready to be sacrificed.
       "Now," he said to the false prophets, "call upon your Gods to light the fire."
       The prophets of Baal danced and chanted for days calling upon the fire to light. It did not.' (1 Kings 18).
11th   St Martin's Day – many good stories are linked to this saint.

Secular occasions

5th   A 'people who help us' theme here could offer good dramatic ideas linked with the London Fire Brigade. Useful starting statistics might be, in the Great fire of London in 1666, 13,200 homes and 89 churches were destroyed and 200,000 people were made homeless.

7th   Marie Sklodowska was born in 1867. After marriage she was Marie Curie, Nobel prize-winner for the discovery of radium with her husband in 1898.

8th   In 1922 Dr Christian Barnard, the first surgeon to transplant a human heart, was born.

12th   In a battle at San Juan in Puerto Rico, a cannonball hit a stool on which Sir Francis Drake was sitting. He was unhurt.

18th   The last load of British convicts was put ashore in Australia in 1840.

22nd   Supposedly Robin Hood died on this day in 1247.

26th   Lewis Carroll finished the manuscript for *Alice in Wonderland* in 1864.

DECEMBER

Religious occasions

CHRISTMAS A different approach to Christmas might be to consider some of the creatures associated with the occasion. The robin supposedly got its red breast through flying low over the fire in the stable and fanning it with its wings.

The raven was supposedly present when the angels appeared to the shepherds. The cockerel was given the task of announcing to the world that Jesus had been born. Its Latin cry – 'Christus natus est' (Christ is born) has a pleasing rhythmic similarity to 'Cock-a doodle-do'.

A cat was supposed to have given birth to a litter of kittens when Jesus was born. The ox and ass were symbols of humility and the camels associated with the wise men symbolised power, wealth and royalty.

HANUKKAH Jewish festival of lights celebrated by lighting candles in the nine-branched menorah; playing with a dreidel; and eating potato pancakes (latkes).

6th   St Nicholas, Bishop of Myra, died in 342.

13th   St Lucia's Day. She helped persecuted Christians.

Secular occasions

5th   Mozart died in 1791.

7th   Pearl Harbor was attacked by Japan, causing the USA to enter the Second World War in 1941.

12th   Marconi's first transatlantic radio message was sent in 1901.

18th   In 1865 slavery was abolished in the USA.

22nd Beatrix Potter, creator of *Peter Rabbit*, died in 1943.

28th   The Lumiere brothers gave the first cinema show in Paris in 1895.

JANUARY

Religious occasions

EPIPHANY the twelfth night after Christmas. Christian celebration of Jesus's presentation to the Magi and symbolic gifts: gold for a king; frankincense for a priest; myrrh for suffering.

5th   This is the feast day of St Simeon Stylites. The son of a Syrian shepherd, born c.390, he spent the last thirty-six years of his life living on a raised platform from which he dispensed prayers and advice.

8th   St Nathalan's Day. When people were starving the Scottish saint sowed sand and, miraculously, it produced a rich harvest crop.

15th   Feast day of St Paul, the first hermit, who died in 342 and was said to have been brought his food by a raven.

Secular occasions

12th   From 576 BC Roman slaves were allowed this day as their one annual day of freedom when they could be their own masters.

16th   The Orient Express made its first journey in 1883.

18th   A 'jazz versus classics' concert was held in the Metropolitan Opera House in New York in 1944.

20th   John F. Kennedy said 'Ask not what your country can do for you; ask what you can do for your country' in his inaugural speech in 1961.

25th   Robert Burns' Night.

26th   Australia Day.

27th   Fire killed the US astronauts in the capsule of an Apollo moon mission in 1967.

FEBRUARY

Religious occasions

CANDLEMAS celebrated on the 2nd, commemorates the presentation of Jesus at the temple. Candles are blessed in churches and distributed to members of the congregation.

SHIVA RATRI Shiva, one of the three most important Hindu gods, is celebrated in dance and drama. Shiva traditionally dances on the back of ignorance, which must be destroyed so that people can be enlightened.

SHROVE TUESDAY commonly called 'Pancake Day', the time for using up fat and eggs before fasting during the forty days of Lent.

ASH WEDNESDAY ashes made from the burnt palm crosses of the previous year are sprinkled with water and blessed, then daubed on the forehead as a sign of repentance.

'Giving' could be a dramatic link involving several of these occasions. For instance, candles which are blessed are given to members of the congregation at Candlemas services; fat and eggs are 'given' in the form of pancakes on Shrove Tuesday; Palm crosses are given on Ash Wednesday. This could be continued to link to March festival when flowers and cards are given to mothers on Mothering Sunday; special food called 'hamantaschen' is given at Purim.

Secular occasions

4th   Charles Lindbergh. First man to fly the Atlantic solo was born in 1902.

7th   It was on this day in 1845 that William Lloyd went into the British Museum and deliberately broke the Portland Vase, the most valuable glass object in the world. It was painstakingly repaired.

11th   This is a day of celebration in Japan to commemorate the founding of the country in 660 BC.

18th   This is the birthday of Sri Rama Krishna (1836). Originally he was a Hindu, then a Muslim, and finally studied Christianity. 'There are many ways to reach the top of a house,' he said, 'so there are different paths to the Almighty.' He believed God was the centre of all religions.

20th   John Glenn, astronaut, was the first American to orbit the earth on this date in 1962.

MARCH

Religions occasions

MOTHERING SUNDAY the fourth Sunday in Lent when children give flowers, cards and presents to their mothers.

PURIM Jewish commemoration of Esther's triumph over Haman with processions, music and plays. Children are encouraged to make rude noises when the name of Haman is mentioned in services. Special food is eaten such as pastries containing poppy seeds called hamantaschen.

HOLI Hindu Spring Festival, a time of high spirits and good humour, expressed by throwing coloured powder over other people as Lord Krishna did.

PALM SUNDAY commemorates Jesus's entry into Jerusalem. People are given palm crosses in church services.

Secular occasions

2nd   John Wesley died in 1791. He preached forty thousand sermons, travelling four hundred thousand kilometres in his life to do so.

3rd   Birth of Alexander Graham Bell (1847), the inventor of the telephone.

12th   In 1935 the 30mph speed limit was introduced to Britain.

23rd   Roger Bannister was born in 1929. He was the first athlete to run a mile in less than four minutes.

29th   This was the date of the last entry in Polar explorer Captain Scott's diary in 1912.

30th   In 1820 Anna Sewell, author of *Black Beauty*, was born.

APRIL

Religious occasions

ASCENSION DAY celebrated with rogation processions and prayers – originally pagan for good crops. Some parishes 'beat the bounds' at this time. In Derbyshire, villagers dress wells with flowers – a custom started by the villagers of Tissington in gratitude for surviving the Black Death of 1350.

15th   Guru Nanak, founder of the Sikh religion, was born on 15th April 1469.

23rd   St George's Day. He is associated with Mummers' plays.

Secular occasions

2nd   Birthdate of Hans Christian Andersen in 1805.

4th   In 1581 Queen Elizabeth I knighted Sir Francis Drake for his round the world voyage.

13th   In 1962 an international agreement was signed by forty countries to stop the pollution of seas and beaches.

15th   Sinking of the *Titanic* in 1912.

15th   Father Damien, friend of lepers, died in 1889.

22nd   In 1794 Edmund Bon became the first qualified vet in Britain.

23rd   Shakespeare's birthday in 1564.

26th   'Blind Jack' Metcalf died in 1810. Despite being blind at six he became a famous road builder.

28th   Voyage of the *Kon-Tiki* began in 1947. Made of balsa wood, Thor Heyerdahl's craft took one hundred and one days to sail the South Pacific to prove ancient Polynesians could have done this.

MAY

Religious occasions

WESAK great Buddhist festival celebrating the birth, enlightenment and death of the Buddha. Festivities last three days – flowers and lanterns decorate buildings; candles are lit; spectacular processions take place; presents are given to the poor; and caged birds are set free.

WHITSUN the fiftieth day after Easter and it celebrates the giving of the Holy Spirit to the followers of Christ. It is also known as Pentecost (this comes from the Greek word for 'fiftieth') and it was from this time that the followers of Jesus began to preach their faith.

Secular occasions

3rd   Margaret Thatcher became the first woman Prime Minister of the UK in 1979.

6th   In 1952 Maria Montessori died. This educationalist believed each child should learn creatively and be treated as an individual.

8th   VE Day in 1945 marked the end of the Second World War in Europe.

15th   In 1928 the Flying Doctor Service began in Australia. It was the idea of a priest called John Flynn.

29th   Edmund Hillary and Tenzing Norgay became the first men to climb Everest in 1953.

JUNE

Religious occasions

SHAVUOTH Jewish Festival of Weeks, summer festival celebrating corn harvest – food for mind and body. Special food is eaten such as cheese fritters called blintzes.

8th   Muhammad, founder of Islam, died in 632.
24th   St John the Baptist's Day.
29th   St Peter's Day.

Secular occasions

8th   1772 Robert Stevenson, builder of lighthouses, was born. He built the famous Bell Rock structure.
9th   1870 Death of Charles Dickens.
16th   In 1963 Valentina Tereshkova was the first woman to travel in space.
18th   In 1918 Michel Quoist was born. His prayers, such as 'Lord I have time', are stimulating and dramatic assembly material.
20th   In 1854 Lieutenant Charles Lucas was awarded the first Victoria Cross. Aboard HMS *Hecla* he threw a live bomb overboard, saving many lives.
27th   Helen Keller born in 1880.

JULY

Religious occasions

15th   St Swithin's Day. A Saxon Bishop of Winchester, he died in 862.
25th   Feast Day of St Christopher, patron saint of travellers.

Secular occasions

4th   American Independence Day in 1776.
5th   In 1948 the National Health Service began in Britain.
20th   In 1969 Neil Armstrong and Edwin Aldrin were the first men on the moon.

Useful quotations

'Make no mistake about it; you will be punished for your sin'
   (Numbers 32:23).

'Human beings must not depend on bread alone to sustain them'
   (Deuteronomy 8:3).

'The value of wisdom is more than coral or crystal or rubies'
   (Job 28:18).

'Joy comes in the morning'
   (Psalms 30:5).

'Happy are those who are concerned for the poor'
   (Psalms 41:1).

'How wonderful it is, how pleasant, for God's people to live together in harmony'
   (Psalms 133:1).

'Wise children make their fathers proud of them; foolish ones bring their mothers grief'
   (Proverbs 10:1).

'When people are happy, they smile'
   (Proverbs 15:13).

'What a joy it is to find just the right word for the right occasion'
   (Proverbs 15:23).

'Those who are sure of themselves do not talk all the time'
   (Proverbs 17:27).

'Teach children how they should live and they will remember it all their lives'
   (Proverbs 22:6).

'A good reputation is better than expensive perfume'
   (Ecclesiastes 7:1).

'Never abandon an old friend'
   (Ecclesiasticus 9:10).

'Love is patient and kind'
   (1 Corinthians 13:4).

'He who bears no ill will to any being will find favour'
(Hindu).

'Different creeds are but different paths to reach the Almighty'
(Hindu).

'All that we are is the result of what we have thought'
(Buddhism).

'Let a man overcome anger by love, evil by good, greed by kindness, lies
by truth'
(Buddhism).

'He who knows others is wise; he who knows himself is enlightened'
(Taoism).

'The Lord requires you to do justice and to love kindness'
(Judaism).

'Who hath taught the use of a pen, hath taught man that which he knew
not'
(Islam).

'Guide us on a straight path'
(Islam).

'Force malice away from your thoughts'
(Zoroastrianism).

'Once a word has been allowed to escape it cannot be recalled'
(Homer).

'Help yourself and heaven will help you'
(Fontaine).

'No one who has not given his mother a smile has ever been thought
worthy'
(Virgil).

'No man can hide his character'
(Confucius).

'With coarse food to eat and water to drink and with no pillow but a
bent arm, I can still find happiness'
(Confucius).

'Follow the three Rs: Respect for self, respect for others and responsibility
for all your actions'
(Tibetan).

'Remember that silence is sometimes the best answer'
(Tibetan).

'A loving atmosphere in your home is the foundation for your life'
(Tibetan).

'Be gentle with the earth'
(Tibetan).

Drama development

This section offers suggestions as to how some of the dramatic starter ideas listed in Ideas for drama can be developed.

81 ARE YOU CONTENT?

This story is based on an old Jewish folk tale and is narrated by various children taking the readings in turn. As the story unfolds, other members of the presenting class act out the actions appropriate to the readings.

SCRIPT: see p 176

82 TO GIVE IS TO RECEIVE

This story is from the Middle East and apart from its moral significance, it is a wonderful mathematical puzzle which intrigues children. The reader/action/mime format works well in this presentation.

SCRIPT: see p 178

83 GREED GETS NOTHING

The third and final tale in this section is from the Far East although very similar versions can be found in Europe. Once again the reader/action format seems suitable.

SCRIPT: see p 181

Scripted plays

This section selects some of the dramatic starter ideas listed in Ideas for drama and provides a fully scripted play for each.

84 THE SILVER LINING

This play relates to the starter idea so named. There are three possible ways in which it could be presented.
1. Readings could be prepared beforehand and then presented live in assembly.
2. The script could be read and taped in the classroom. This could then be amplified in the assembly while the presenters mimed the action.
3. The reading of the script could be supplemented by a series of pictures on an overhead projector relating to the action as it happened.

CHARACTERS: Dad, Nadia, Mum, doctor and ballet teacher.

Teacher's note – Nadia Nerina became world famous as the prima ballerina of the Royal Ballet.

SCRIPT: see p 183

85 GIFTS

This play is based on an old European folk tale and the theme is the gift of good health. As with the other plays, the presentation can be made in a manner which appeals most to teacher and pupils.

CHARACTERS: King Osric, Svenson (the King's chief servant), various other servants, cook, narrator.

ESSENTIAL PROP: a mirror.

SCRIPT: see p 186

86 MODESTY

This is a simple little play with a strong message.

CHARACTERS: Jocasta, her mother, a magic bird, Gretchen (a jealous, unpleasant girl), Gretchen's mother, various villagers.

SCRIPT: see p 189

Assembly scripts

71 CHOOSING A PATH

The music is played as the audience enters

SPEAKER 1   Every day of our lives we make journeys. Let's look at some of them.

Two pupils move to the front of the presentation area

PUPIL 1   When you think about it, we are always making journeys in school.

PUPIL 2   Yes, we have to go to the classroom from the playground when we come in.

PUPIL 1   And from the classroom to the hall for music, PE and assembly.

PUPIL 2   And to the library.

PUPIL 1   And the dining hall.

PUPIL 2   Even in the classroom we make tiny journeys to the book area.

PUPIL 1   And the sink.

PUPIL 2   And the computers.

SPEAKER 1   Then at the end of the school day, we make a journey home.

Two more pupils come forward

PUPIL 3   How do you get home from school?

PUPIL 4   I go in my mum's car.

PUPIL 3   I walk.

PUPIL 4   We both have to use the crossing patrol to get safely across the road though.

PUPIL 3   And we are both helped by the traffic lights.

PUPIL 4   My mum has to know the way in the car.

PUPIL 3   I have to know the way too!

SPEAKER 1   Here is a map of the local area. Everybody can see their way to and from school if they look carefully at it afterwards. Maps help us on journeys.

SPEAKER 2   That's right, maps do help us on journeys. But there is another important journey we all make.

SPEAKER 1   Oh, what's that?

SPEAKER 2   It is the journey we all make through life.

SPEAKER 1   That's not always an easy journey, is it?

SPEAKER 2   No, it has its ups and downs like most journeys. But you know there are things like maps to help us here too.

SPEAKER 1   Really?

SPEAKER 2   Yes, look.

Eight pupils come forward from the presenters and each carries a placard with the word 'RIGHT' printed on it.

SPEAKER 3   One of the great religions of the world is Buddhism. Buddhists believe that the way to contentment in life is to follow an eightfold path. Each of these paths tells us how we should live. Look and listen.

The first placard holder holds their card above their head

HOLDER 1   We must have the right understanding of life and see it as it is and not how we would like it to be.

The second placard holder holds their card above their head

HOLDER 2   We must have the right thoughts.

The third placard holder holds their card above their head

HOLDER 3   We must have the right speech with no lies or cruel words.

The fourth placard holder holds their card above their head

HOLDER 4   We must have the right action – kindness and honesty.

The fifth placard holder holds their card above their head

HOLDER 5   We must have the right job – something which does no harm to anyone else.

The sixth placard holder holds their card above their head

HOLDER 6   We must have the right effort to try to find new ways to do good.

The seventh placard holder holds their card above their head

HOLDER 7   We must have the right mindfulness in our feelings about things.

The eighth placard holder holds their card above their head

HOLDER 8   We must have the right concentration to help us think and understand.

SPEAKER 1   So now we know we can get some help in our journey through life.

SPEAKER 2   Bow your heads for our prayer.

SPEAKER 1   Let us think this morning about our own journey through life. Let us hope and pray that as we get older, we get wiser. Let us pray that we have the strength to deal with disappointment and misfortune. Let us pray that we can do as much good as we possibly can as we journey through life. Amen.

HYMN: 'The journey of life' No 45 *The Complete Come and Praise*

72 SPECIAL PEOPLE

After the audience is seated, music accompanies the presenting class into the hall. The presenters form a semicircle facing the audience. Pupils who have a book or photograph to show stand slightly forward in the middle of the semicircle.

PUPIL 1   We have collected some books and photographs to show you.

PUPIL 2   They are all about famous people.

Pupil 3 holds up their book

PUPIL 3   This book tells us about [subjects in the book].

Pupil 4 holds up their book

PUPIL 4   This book tells us about [subjects in the book].

Pupil 5 holds up their book

PUPIL 5   This book tells us about [subjects in the book].

PUPIL 6   Now look at these photographs.

Pupil 7 holds up their photograph

PUPIL 7   Here is a famous [e.g. politician].

Pupil 8 holds up their photograph

PUPIL 8   Here is a famous [e.g. writer].

Pupil 9 holds up their photograph

PUPIL 9   Here is a famous [e.g. sportsperson].

PUPIL 10   The Bible tells us that we should remember and praise people who have . . .

PUPIL 11   Been great kings.

PUPIL 12   Given good advice.

PUPIL 13   Written great music or words.

PUPIL 14   Been kind and generous to others.

Two pupils, apparently in conversation and indifferent to everybody else, interrupt

Good Morning Everybody Book 2 © Redvers Brandling, Nelson Thornes Ltd, 2002

PUPIL 15   All this talk about special people. I think we're all special.

PUPIL 16   How do you mean?

PUPIL 15   Well, we all look different, we sound different, we're good at different things . . .

PUPIL 16   I see what you mean but . . .

The teacher asks everybody to bow their heads for a prayer, which embodies the thoughts of the assembly

TEACHER   Every single life is a special one. We have all been given qualities to make us special. It is how we use these qualities which is so important. Do we always do our very best? Are we kind and helpful, thoughtful and considerate? Do we use what we are good at to give pleasure to others? Dear God help us to realise that we are all special people and help us to behave so that others will think so. Amen.

HYMN: the choice is so wide here that every teacher will have their own idea of what this should be

73 BELONGING TO A COMMUNITY

The audience is allowed to enter and take its place before the presenters appear. The focal point is the 'wall' which has been constructed in the presenting area. The presenters take up positions on either side of the wall and make loud comments about it

PUPIL 1   I expect everybody's wondering what this is here for.

PUPIL 2   It's a special wall isn't it?

PUPIL 3   There's a story about this wall.

PUPIL 4   Shall we tell it now?

PUPIL 5   No, let's wait a few minutes.

PUPIL 6   Why?

PUPIL 7   Well, we've got something else to say first.

By this time all the presenters should be in place and a speaker continues

SPEAKER   Before we talk about the wall, we want everybody to think about belonging to something.

PUPIL 8   What do you mean by belonging?

PUPIL 9   Belonging to what?

SPEAKER   Well, we all belong to this school. We all belong to our families. We might belong to organisations such as the Cubs, or Brownies, or a football team, or dancing class or drama group.

PUPIL 10   It's fun to belong to groups like this.

PUPIL 11   We often belong to groups because we like doing the same things.

SPEAKER   If you belong to something you are part of a community. It is often fun and you know that the other people in the community will help you. It is marvellous to be able to share activities, experiences and sometimes beliefs.

PUPIL 12   What do you mean by beliefs?

PUPIL 13   I suppose you're going to get round to telling us about the wall now.

Good Morning Everybody Book 2 © Redvers Brandling, Nelson Thornes Ltd, 2002

SPEAKER   Yes, I am. Long, long ago in a city called Jerusalem a king called Solomon built a great temple. There, the people of the Jewish community went to worship God. But, sadly, the enemies of the Jews destroyed the temple. It was rebuilt but then it was destroyed again. Today, all that is left of that temple is a wall of huge stone blocks.
            This wall is one of the most famous in the world. It is called the Wailing Wall. People of the Jewish community travel from all over the world to pray at the Wailing Wall.

When the speaker has finished, some members of the presenting group approach the wall to pray.

SPEAKER   Next, we want you to look at something else.

A pupil steps forward and holds up a jar of water

SPEAKER   If you saw a jar of water like this in a Hindu home, it might be very special water from the River Ganges. Every year, thousands of Hindus go to the city of Benares in India and bathe in the Ganges.
PUPIL 14   Who are Hindus?
PUPIL 15   Why do they do that?
SPEAKER   Hindus believe that a god called Shiva made every-thing. They also believe that when the Ganges was made, the water rushed down from heaven very dangerously. The god Shiva caught the water in his hair so that the people and the earth would not be destroyed. Now when Hindus go to the Ganges they pray for forgiveness for what they have done wrong and they throw flowers in the river.
PUPIL 16   What about people with other beliefs?
PUPIL 17   What about their communities?
SPEAKER   Well, let's look at some pictures as we answer these questions.

A succession of pupils display pictures, artefacts and placards relating to churches and mosques

Good Morning Everybody Book 2 © Redvers Brandling, Nelson Thornes Ltd, 2002

SPEAKER   People who are Christians go to church. [Further comment relating to what is shown.]

SPEAKER   People who are Muslims worship in a mosque. [Further comment relating to what is shown.]

TEACHER   This morning we have thought about belonging to a community. We all belong to the community of this school. We all belong to our families. Depending on what we believe, we might belong to different communities such as Jews, Christians, Hindus or Muslims.

Whatever community we belong to we know that it means sharing things with other people. Bow your heads while we listen to some words written by a boy. They are about sharing.

I couldn't bear to think
That
There wasn't
Anybody
Anywhere
Who cared, just a bit
About me.
I couldn't bear to think
That
There wasn't
Somebody
Somewhere
Who shared my hopes,
My fears,
My joy,
My tears.   S. Simpson.

HYMN: 'You can build a wall' No 91 *The Complete Come and Praise*

74 COLOUR, COLOUR, COLOUR

The presenting class should be in position before the audience enters the hall

SPEAKER 1	Good morning everybody. Today in our assembly we are going to think about colour. Now we are . . .

A pupil walks across to the speaker and interrupts

PUPIL 1	Just a minute, just a minute!
SPEAKER 1	What is it? You're interrupting here.
PUPIL 1	Did I hear you mentioning colour?
SPEAKER 1	Yes, you did, but . . .
PUPIL 1	Have you thought about how important colours are in our everyday lives?
SPEAKER 1	Well . . .
PUPIL 1	Just think. The red, green and amber of traffic lights keep us safe on the roads; our clothes are different colours; our hair and eyes are different colours; and our houses are painted different colours. There's just colour all around us.

Three pupils come forward and each waves the appropriate symbol

PUPIL 2	I'm a football fan and this is the colour of my favourite football team.
PUPIL 3	These are the colours in our school uniform.
PUPIL 4	I like motor racing and this is the black and white chequered flag which is waved to end a race.
SPEAKER 2	Colours are important in nature too. For instance . . .
PUPIL 5	The fields and trees are green.
PUPIL 6	The snow in winter is white.
PUPIL 7	Flowers are all different colours.
PUPIL 8	Animals use colours for camouflage.
PUPIL 9	Some creatures change colour as they grow from babies to adults.
PUPIL 10	Rainbows are multicoloured.

Good Morning Everybody Book 2 © Redvers Brandling, Nelson Thornes Ltd, 2002

PUPIL 11   Tigers are orange with black stripes.

SPEAKER 3   We think of colours in connection with other things too.

Two pupils come to the front of the stage

SPEAKER 3   When a couple get married, the bride often wears white. They might wear gold or silver wedding rings.

The couple hold up wedding rings

SPEAKER 3   In the Christian church, gold and white are also the colours for Christmas and Easter. Red is the colour for saints' days. Red is the colour of the Hindu festival of Holi. Diwali, another festival, has many colours.

A pupil holding cymbals brings them together with a great crash

CYMBAL   We could go on and on telling you about colours.
PLAYER   They are beautiful and they are everywhere.

The other members of the presenting group all move round in a circle. Each pupil holds up a coloured card or piece of paper

CYMBAL   Now stop again. Bow your heads and listen to the
PLAYER   words of this prayer.
            Let us think this morning of the wonder, joy and beauty of colours. Let us give thanks for them making our world a brighter, more marvellous place.

HYMN: 'For the beauty of the earth' No 11 *The Complete Come and Praise*

75 SETTING AN EXAMPLE

Once the audience is in position, most of the presenting class enter and take their places. A small group follow bringing a book wrapped in cloth (the Qur'an), a book stand and a bowl of water. Once these have been set in a prominent position, a series of pupils call out statements as those who have brought in artefacts carry out appropriate actions

PUPIL 1   This is the Muslim holy book.

PUPIL 2   It is called the Qur'an.

PUPIL 3   A copy of this book is kept in Muslim homes.

PUPIL 4   It is carefully wrapped in a cloth.

PUPIL 5   It is kept on a high shelf above all other books.

PUPIL 6   No one is allowed to touch it without washing their hands first.

SPEAKER 1   Muhammad is the man who founded the Muslim religion. He was an orphan at six years old. He looked after goats and camels. As he grew up he spent a lot of time thinking. One day he felt he had been visited by an angel who told him that God wanted him to show people how to live. The angel told him about the book which would help him and all the people. This was the Qur'an.

SPEAKER 2   So Muhammad started to ask people to become Muslims. This meant being kind to each other and helping those in trouble. But many people did not want to change. One night, Muhammad was resting after a long journey. Some other men were with him. One of these men hated Muhammad. Watch and see what happened.

Several men lie sleeping. One of them, Rachid, gets to his feet and speaks

RACHID   This Muhammad is making my life too difficult. He says I should free my slaves! I'm going to put an end to him once and for all.

Good Morning Everybody Book 2 © Redvers Brandling, Nelson Thornes Ltd, 2002

Rachid draws his sword, advances to the sleeping Muhammad and puts the sword to his neck. Muhammad wakes with a start

MUHAMMAD What are you doing?

RACHID   I'm going to kill you. Nobody can save you now.

MUHAMMAD You're forgetting that Allah can save me Rachid. He doesn't want you to kill me.

RACHID   What?

In Rachid's confusion, Muhammad leaps up, wrenches the sword from his grasp and brings the point to bear on his throat

RACHID   Spare me! Spare me, Muhammad.

MUHAMMAD Yes, I will spare you, Rachid, and forgive you too. But remember what Allah has taught us; do only to others what you would like them to do to you.

SPEAKER 1 And so Rachid was forgiven. He had learnt his lesson. He became a Muslim and tried to help everyone he met.

SPEAKER 2 We have seen in our assembly this morning that some people can inspire others by the way they behave.

SPEAKER 1 You probably already know somebody who has made a difference to your life by the things they do and the example they set.

PUPIL 7   It may be your mum . . .

PUPIL 8   Or your dad . . .

PUPIL 9   Or one of your teachers . . .

PUPIL 10   Or a friend.

SPEAKER 2 Bow your heads for our prayer. Let us give thanks this morning for all those people who set us good examples of how to behave. Teach us to think before we act and to try always to be as kind, helpful and thoughtful as possible.

HYMN: 'The family of Man' No 69 *The Complete Come and Praise*

76 STORIES AT CHRISTMAS

The presenting class welcome the audience and a reader takes up a prominent position at the side. As they read the text, the scene is enacted by pupils playing the various parts. While the action is taking place, the rest of the group sing 'We three kings' softly

READER 1   Long ago three kings saw a star. They followed it to the stable where Jesus was born.

Kings make a circuit of the hall

READER 1   A little girl knew what the kings were doing and she followed them.

Little girl following some distance behind the kings

READER 1   Eventually the kings reached the stable. Each was carrying a gift. They went inside to give their gifts to the new-born king.

Kings go inside the stable

READER 1   The little girl followed them to the stable door. She saw them go inside with their gifts. But she had nothing to give. She was so sad that she started to cry. As each of her tears fell to the ground, it turned into a beautiful rose. Bending down, she picked up the roses and went into the stable. Now she had a present to give too.

READER 2   This was the story that has grown up about the Christmas rose. Another plant which is linked to Christmas is the Glastonbury thorn. Listen to its story.

Another pupils moves across the stage with a staff and performs the actions

READER 2   There was a man called Joseph of Arimathea who was a secret follower of Jesus. He came to England to tell the story of Jesus and he travelled to Glastonbury. There an amazing thing happened.

Good Morning Everybody Book 2 © Redvers Brandling, Nelson Thornes Ltd, 2002

He stuck his staff in the ground and it immediately took root. Then flowers appeared on it on Christmas day in honour of Jesus's birth. So a great Christian church was built at Glastonbury.

ALL   Christmas is indeed a very special time.
Christmas is a time for giving.
Christmas is a time for families.
Christmas is a time for singing.
Christmas is a time for giving thanks.
Christmas is a time for thinking.
Christmas is a time for praying.
Christmas is a time for fun.
Christmas is a time for remembering.

READER 2   So many lovely words help us to remember and celebrate Christmas. Listen to this poem.

READER 3   Wind through the olive trees
Softly did blow,
Round little Bethlehem
Long, long ago.

Sheep on the hillside lay
Whiter than snow;
Shepherds were watching them
Long, long ago.

Then from the happy sky,
Angels bent low,
Singing their songs of joy
Long, long ago.

For in a manger bed,
Cradled we know,
Christ came to Bethlehem
Long, long ago.   (Anon)

HYMN: 'Mary had a baby' No 123 *The Complete Come and Praise*

77 GOOD TIMES AND BAD

The presenting class are already in position in their coats when the audience comes in to the music/sound effects.

SPEAKER 1 Winter – a time of cold.

SPEAKER 2 And darkness.

SPEAKER 3 And sometimes dangerous roads and seas.

SPEAKER 1 A time when people get more coughs and colds.

SPEAKER 2 A time when life is often hard and worrying for old people.

SPEAKER 3 A time when life is very hard for some creatures.

SPEAKER 1 Now listen to this poem.

ALL Winter,
A beautiful time?
Not to the birds,
They don't think so.

Swirling,
Above the trees,
Ready to fly
And eager to go.

Empty,
Hard, blue sky
Over grasping trees
Awaiting snow.

Winter,
Spring on its heels.
Don't tell the birds,
They already know.

SPEAKER 1 If we think about the poem we have just heard, we are reminded that winter is often cruel to birds but we see by the end of the poem that they already know that the hope of spring is not far away.

Good Morning Everybody Book 2 © Redvers Brandling, Nelson Thornes Ltd, 2002

SPEAKER 2	In some ways our lives are like the seasons. Just as the birds dread winter we hate disappointments and worrying things. Here are some of them.
PUPIL 1	I was really disappointed when we couldn't go on holiday.
PUPIL 2	I hated having the flu. I thought I would never feel better.
PUPIL 3	It was awful when my mum had to go in to hospital. We were all worried about her and home didn't seem the same at all.
PUPIL 4	Everybody else got their maths right but I couldn't do mine.
PUPIL 5	When I first had to wear glasses I hated it because the other girls teased me.
PUPIL 6	When I first went to school I was lonely and some boys bullied me.
SPEAKER 1	Just as the birds know that spring follows winter we must remember that there are good times as well as those which are disappointing, difficult and worrying. A famous saint wrote a prayer to remind us of this.
SPEAKER 2	We are going to take our coats off to remind us that there is warmth as well as cold and then we are going to listen to this prayer.

The pupils all remove their coats

ALL	We are going to read a prayer by St Francis because we have been thinking about birds and animals and he is their patron saint. Here is his prayer: Where there is hatred, let there be love. Where there is doubt, faith, Where there is despair, hope, Where there is darkness, light, Where there is sadness, joy.

HYMN: 'Lord of hopefulness' No 52 *The Complete Come and Praise*

78 IT MAKES ME THINK

The presenting class are already in position as the audience enter

SPEAKER 1   Good morning everybody. This morning we are going to begin by showing you some words which will make you have very pleasant thoughts. Look.

Several pupils come to the front of the presenting class with placards. These are initially kept hidden and then, one after the other, they are turned round to show the words 'chocolate', 'holidays', etc.

SPEAKER 2   These words make us think about things we enjoy. Here are some more things which make particular people think and enjoy what they suggest.

Three pairs of children come to the front. There is a boy and a girl in each pairing and each girl carries with her red and gold thread. The pairs perform the actions described

SPEAKER 3   In India, there is a lovely festival called Raksha Bandhan. It takes place once a year and sisters tie red and gold thread round the wrists of their brothers. 'Raksha' means 'to protect' and 'Bandhan' means 'to tie'. By doing this, the sisters seek to protect their brothers from any harm or evil during the year. The brothers in turn promise to protect their sisters.

They are replaced by another group, comprising a speaker and several pupils holding pictures of firework activity

SPEAKER 4   We all enjoy fireworks. But if you are a Hindu, you look forward particularly to the festival of Dassehra. This celebrates the goddess Durga and on the last day there is a great carnival procession including huge images of the demon king Ravana, which are filled with crackers and fireworks. Arrows of fire are shot into them. You can imagine the bangs and the colours! This is to celebrate that good has beaten evil once again!

They are replaced by another group, containing several pupils who have party noise-makers

SPEAKER 5   If you are a Jewish child you look forward to Purim. At this festival, the story of how Queen Esther saved the people from the evil Haman is celebrated. Haman wanted the Jews destroyed but Esther pleaded with the king and in the end it was Haman who was hanged. When this story is read in the synagogue, the children make a terrific noise whenever the name of the villain 'Haman' is mentioned.

They are replaced by another group. Three pupils in this group should carry placards showing the numbers '7', '5' and '3'

SPEAKER 6   There is a very old festival in Japan called Shichi-go-shan. The words stand for the numbers ' 7–5–3' and on this festival Japanese parents go to the temple to give thanks that their children have reached these ages safely. They then pray for their futures.

TEACHER   This morning we have heard lots of words and actions which remind us of the good things in our lives and the thoughtful, caring things which many do for others. Let us pray that our own words and actions are always those which other people will enjoy and appreciate.

79 FACTS OF A DISASTER

SPEAKER   Good morning everybody. Now we are going back in time to the year 1861. The date is August 25th and we are at Brighton railway station. Look there are three trains waiting to travel to London.

The speaker points to one side of the presenting area to the three trains

TRAIN A   I am Train A.
PUPIL 1   Train A set off for London.

Train A chugs slowly round the hall

TRAIN B   I am Train B.
PUPIL 2   Train B left for London seven minutes later. It was full.

Train B chugs out. Immediately it does so a pupil runs out and holds up a 'MISTAKE' placard

PUPIL 3   This was a mistake. The second train should have waited for another fourteen minutes!
TRAIN C   I am Train C.
PUPIL 4   Train C left for London seven minutes later. It was full.

Train C chugs out after Train B. Immediately another pupil rushes out and holds up a 'MISTAKE' placard

PUPIL 5   This was another mistake. Train C should have waited for fourteen minutes after Train B left.

All three trains are chugging slowly round the hall. A signal operator stands at the entrance to the tunnel. Train A goes in slowly and stays until another pupil rushes out and holds up a 'MISTAKE' placard

PUPIL 6   This was another mistake. The 'Danger – Train in Tunnel' signal should now have showed. It failed because it was not working.

Good Morning Everybody Book 2 © Redvers Brandling, Nelson Thornes Ltd, 2002

SPEAKER   When the signal did not work, Henry the signal operator was horrified when he saw Train B coming. He grabbed his red flag for danger and waved to Train B to stop. It couldn't stop quickly enough and slowly entered the tunnel.

Train B goes slowly into the tunnel and as it does so Train A leaves at the other end and chugs out

SPEAKER   Henry did not know that the driver of Train B had seen his red flag. So he rushed to his signal box and sent a message to the other end – 'Is the tunnel clear?' The signalman at the other end of the tunnel had just seen Train A leave so he signalled back – 'Tunnel clear'.

Another pupil rushes out and holds up a 'MISTAKE' placard

PUPIL 7   This was a terrible mistake. Both signal operators think the tunnel is clear, but it is not! Train B had managed to stop after seeing the red flag and it is still in the tunnel!

SPEAKER   Henry then saw Train C coming, again fourteen minutes earlier than it should have been . . .

Without comment another 'MISTAKE' placard is produced

SPEAKER   Thinking the tunnel was clear, Henry waved his white flag to say the tunnel was clear and it was safe to go through.

Another 'MISTAKE' placard appears

SPEAKER   Train C rushed into the tunnel and . . .

Tremendous crashing from cymbals and drums in the tunnel. Shouts and screams from the pupils

SPEAKER   A terrible crash had taken place in the tunnel and many people were hurt.

TEACHER   This was a terrible disaster. It happened because the rules for safety were not obeyed. The trains should have left with twenty-one minutes between each of them. They only allowed seven minutes. The signal at the entrance to the tunnel did not work properly. As a result, the signal operator waved the wrong flag. It was later found that Henry had been on duty for twenty-four hours instead of eight!

Now bow your heads and listen to our prayer.

Let us pray this morning that we are always sensible about obeying rules of safety. When we lift our heads let us look at the word in front of us. Let us be sure what it means and why it is important.

Good Morning Everybody Book 2 © Redvers Brandling, Nelson Thornes Ltd, 2002

80 SPECIAL DAYS

A group dressed as miners move to the front of the presenting area.
They carry a banner depicting a mining scene

SPEAKER   Here you see some miners. It is the third Saturday
in July and they are walking to Durham. Ever
since 1871, miners have had a great festival in the
city on this day. Now mining has almost disappeared but the festival was a very great occasion
with marching, music, fun and prayers in the
cathedral. It was a special day for everybody con-
nected with coal-mines.

The miners move back and another pupil moves forward carrying
a clock whose hands are set at midnight

SPEAKER   Midnight. At the great Hindu festival of
Janmashtami, this is a very special time because
Hindus believe the great god Krishna was born at
midnight. There are presents, special food, singing
and dancing at this time.

The clock group are replaced by another group who come to the
front and perform a country dance of some sort (a Morris dance
would be ideal)

SPEAKER   Dancing like this was very popular at the festival
of Whitsun. Whit Sunday is sometimes described
as the birthday of the Christian church. This is
because it was on this day that the disciples were
given the power to continue the work Jesus had
started.

Another group of children come to the front, each bearing a lantern

SPEAKER   A great lantern festival called Teng Chieh is held
in China on the first full moon of the new year.
This festival celebrates the birth of the world and
to give thanks for lighter days and nights to come.

Good Morning Everybody Book 2 © Redvers Brandling, Nelson Thornes Ltd, 2002

The lantern bearers return to the presenting group and are replaced by a new group, each wearing, or carrying, something related to the special days they are going to comment on

PUPIL 1	We have special days in our school life . . .
PUPIL 2	Like the day of the school trip,
PUPIL 3	And Sports Day,
PUPIL 4	And the Christmas party.
PUPIL 5	We have special days in our own lives . . . .
PUPIL 6	Like birthdays,
PUPIL 7	And brothers and sisters' birthdays,
PUPIL 8	And holidays.
PUPIL 9	In fact for someone, somewhere, every single day is a special day.

These pupils return to the presenting group

SPEAKER   Let us give thanks for the special gift of every single day. Let us pray that we may always use our days wisely and also enjoy them as fully as we can. Teach us to be appreciative in all our work and play.

The assembly concludes with everybody singing 'Thank you, Lord' No 32 *The Complete Come and Praise*.

Good Morning Everybody Book 2 © Redvers Brandling, Nelson Thornes Ltd, 2002

Story scripts

81 ARE YOU CONTENT?

READER 1   Isaac was a poor Jewish farmer. He and his family lived in a one-roomed hut. Apart from Isaac and his wife there were one . . . two . . . three . . . four . . . five . . . six children and only one very big bed!

Action portrays the turmoil of the crowded room. Plenty of noise, hustle and bustle

READER 2   There was so much shuffling, shifting, pushing and talking that Isaac became irritated.
'I can't get a decent sleep and I can't even think properly. I'll go and ask the rabbi for his advice,' thought Isaac and so off he went.

Isaac walks out and arrives at the rabbi's house

READER 3   When Isaac arrived at the rabbi's house he poured out his troubles.
'So you see what I mean, Rabbi,' he said. 'What do you suggest?'
'Ah,' replied the rabbi. 'Have you any hens?'
'Well, yes I have,' replied Isaac.
'Good,' continued the rabbi. 'Bring them into the house with you.'
Isaac went home and brought half a dozen hens into the house too.

Pupils dressed as hens cause more chaos

READER 4   And so things in Isaac's house became worse! Off he went to the rabbi again and complained. After thinking hard, the rabbi told him to bring the family goat into the house with him. Isaac returned home and did this. Can you imagine what it was like?

Action showing the commotion caused by the goat

READER 5   Isaac was in despair. He returned to the rabbi again and was astonished when the rabbi advised him to bring the family cow into the house as well! However, he went home and did this.

Action showing all humans and animals in small space causing absolute chaos

READER 6   This time Isaac was really desperate. He rushed back to the rabbi almost in tears. The rabbi stroked his chin and appeared to think for a very long time. Then he spoke.
'Go home and put the hens, the goat and the cow outside.'
So Isaac returned home and did this. It was marvellous! It seemed almost tranquil. And Isaac and his wife began to enjoy each other's company and be content and grateful for what they had.

Action revealing the new realisation and contentment in the household

Good Morning Everybody Book 2 © Redvers Brandling, Nelson Thornes Ltd, 2002

82 TO GIVE IS TO RECEIVE

READER 1   Ali was an Arab chief. He had crossed the desert hundreds of times with his great camel train. Now, however, he was old and lay dying in his tent. His servants fussed over him sadly. Ali called out and at once his chief servant rushed up to him.
'Master, your wish is my command.'
'My friend,' whispered Ali in a weak voice, 'make sure my brother gets this.'

The characters in the tableau should be frozen in positions to depict the key features of the passage

READER 2   A few days later several people gathered together in another tent at the camp. Among those present were Ali's three sons. Various servants stood near the doorway and they ushered in an important-looking man. In his hand he carried the parchment scroll the dying Ali had given to his servant. He nodded to the three sons.
'Your father's will. It is rather unusual. Listen to what it says.'
Opening the scroll, the man, who was Ali's brother read slowly.
'My greatest possessions are my camels and this is how they will be divided between my sons. My eldest son will receive half of the camels; my second son will receive one third of the camels; and my youngest son will have one ninth of the camels.'
Putting the scroll to one side, the uncle clapped his hands.
'Let's go outside and count the camels.'

The camels are counted aloud and the total (seventeen camels) should be repeated loudly

Good Morning Everybody Book 2 © Redvers Brandling, Nelson Thornes Ltd, 2002

READER 3   When the camels were collected they were counted three times to make sure they were all there. When this had been done the eldest son looked puzzled.

'Seventeen camels,' he said. 'How can you have half of seventeen camels?'

The middle son said, 'How can you have one third of seventeen camels?'

Finally, the youngest son said, 'How can you have one ninth of seventeen camels?'

The confused sons scratch their heads and disagree over the impossible division sums

READER 4   'Stop!'

The uncle suddenly brought all the fussing to a halt.

'There are five words at the bottom of your father's will. They say: 'to give is to receive.'

Now I've thought about this. To make the division of the camels possible I'm going to give you one of mine. That will make eighteen to be shared out.'

Another camel is brought in to supplement the herd

READER 5   'So the eldest son took half of the camels, which meant there were nine left.

The youngest son took his third of eighteen, which was six. Next the youngest son took his one ninth of the eighteen camels, which was two.

Now this was very strange! When the sons added up the number of camels they now had – it was seventeen! Now there was one left over!

The camels are shared out, reinforcing the point that there is one left over

READER 6   Once again the uncle held up his hand to stop the confusion. As he did so the youngest son called out in a puzzled voice.

'What shall we do with the one that's left over?'

Good Morning Everybody Book 2 © Redvers Brandling, Nelson Thornes Ltd, 2002

The uncle smiled.

'Well, remember what your father's last words were – to give is to receive.'

'Of course,' said the eldest son. 'Now you must have back the camel that is left as proof of my father's wise words.'

83 GREED GETS NOTHING

READER 1   There was once a poor traveller who was making a long journey. As was usual in his country, the sun scorched down and he was hot and tired.
Eventually he found a tree and sat beneath its shade to eat his only meal of the day. Because he was so poor, the only food he had with him was a smattering of rice and boiled vegetables.

Action from the traveller miming fatigue, heat and hunger. He sits and finishes his meal

READER 2   Just a little way up the road from where the poor traveller was eating his meal was a food stall. This was by the side of the road and the stallholder, an unfriendly-looking man, was frying fish to sell at his stall. He watched the traveller eat and, when he had finished, the stallholder called him over.

Action shows the stallholder at work and ends with the confrontation between the two men

READER 3   When the traveller reached the food stall the stall owner said to him, 'Right, where's my money?'
'What do you mean?' gasped the astonished traveller. 'I haven't bought anything from you.'
'Ah, but you've been smelling my fish all the time you were eating. That made your food taste better so you owe me a silver crown.'
By now a crowd had gathered to listen to the argument.

Action shows a crowd gathering

READER 4   As the two men argued, one of the crowd suddenly shouted out.
'Hey look here's a wise man coming along the road. Why doesn't he decide who's right and who's wrong here?'

Good Morning Everybody Book 2 © Redvers Brandling, Nelson Thornes Ltd, 2002

A wise man enters and the crowd beckons him over with lots of hand-waving and gesticulation to indicate the dilemma

READER 5   For a long time the wise man pondered in silence. Then he gazed up at the sky.

'The stallholder is right,' he said. 'A price must be paid for the smell of the fish.'

'But a silver crown is all the money I have in the world,' pleaded the miserable traveller.

'Come here both of you,' said the wise man. 'Now take that silver crown out of your pocket and hold it out in the sunshine.'

When the traveller had done this the wise man spoke to the stallholder.

'Do you see the shadow of the silver coin?'

'Yes,' replied the mystified stallholder.

'Good,' went on the wise man, 'because the payment for the smell of your fish is to see the shadow of a silver coin.'

Action shows relief from the traveller, fury from the stallholder and amusement and admiration from the crowd

Scripted plays

84 THE SILVER LINING

SCENE 1 A summer's day at home

DAD	Well, I'm glad to be back from work. Hello, Nadia.
NADIA	Hi, Dad. Will you play in the garden with me?
MUM	You go and play in the garden, Nadia. I'll give you a shout when tea's ready.
NADIA	I wonder if I can hop up and down all these garden steps. I'll try one foot then the other and I'll try and go round this huge flowerpot.
DAD	What's for tea today?
MUM	It's one of your favourites . . .
NADIA	Help!
MUM	What?
DAD	Quick, she sounds hurt!

They rush out. Nadia is lying on the garden steps. Her foot is trapped under a flowerpot

MUM	Nadia, what have you done?
NADIA	Oh, Mum . . . I was hopping round the flowerpot and I caught my foot under it and it hurts!
DAD	It looks like a sprained ankle. We'll have to take you straight to the doctor.

SCENE 2 At the doctor's surgery

MUM	It's a long wait, isn't it? Are you all right, Nadia?
NADIA	Oh, it hurts so much!

DAD	Our turn at last. Come on, Nadia, we'll carry you.
DOCTOR	What have we here?
DAD	It's her ankle, doctor . . . .
DOCTOR	Yes, I can see that. Let me feel it. Hmm, it's very swollen and I'm afraid it is very badly sprained. You'll need to take lots of rest, Nadia.

SCENE 3 A month later at home

MUM	I'm still worried about Nadia.
DAD	Yes, I know what you mean. She still can't walk properly and she's lost all her confidence.
MUM	Poor little girl. Nadia, do you want to play in the garden?
NADIA	No thanks, Mum. I'm tired and my ankle hurts.
DAD	Does it still hurt when you walk?
NADIA	Yes. All the time, Dad, and it's still throbbing.
DAD	I'm going to phone the doctor and see what he suggests.
MUM	I'm sure he'll have some ideas on how to make it better.

Dad returns from telephoning the doctor

DAD	Well, he's certainly given me one idea.
MUM	Come on, let's hear it.
DAD	He suggests you have some dancing lessons to strengthen the ankle.
NADIA	Dancing lessons! That sounds great. I'd love to learn ballet.

SCENE 4 At the ballet school three months later

BALLET TEACHER	Nadia, can you go through those exercises again.
NADIA	Yes! I enjoy them.

Nadia does some exercises/dancing

TEACHER	How is the ankle now?

NADIA   It's so long since it hurt I can hardly remember which one it was.

TEACHER   That's great. You know of all the pupils I've had you're the one who has worked hardest of all.

NADIA   I can't tell you how much I've enjoyed it. I never want to do anything but dance in my whole life.

TEACHER   Only the very best dancers make a living from it I'm afraid. Here's your mum and dad.

DAD   Hello, Miss Smyth. How's she getting on?

TEACHER   If you really want to know, let's go over here for a minute.

Teacher leads parents away from Nadia so she can't hear

MUM   Oh dear, is there a problem?

TEACHER   Far from it Mrs Nerina. I have never known a little girl work as hard as your daughter and to think she had such a bad ankle to start with. She really is developing into an exceptional dancer.

DAD   And all because of a sprained ankle.

TEACHER   That might have been the start but it has been sheer courage and determination which has made her as good as she is.

Good Morning Everybody Book 2 © Redvers Brandling, Nelson Thornes Ltd, 2002

85   GIFTS

SCENE 1 The king's palace

READER	King Osric was very handsome young man. He was tall and strong but . . .
KING	Cook! Where are you?
COOK	Here, your majesty.
KING	This pie is delicious. Bring me another helping at once. And after that make sure there's lots of my favourite pudding.
COOK	At once, your majesty.
KING	Servant!
SERVANT 1	Your majesty.
KING	After my lunch I want to look round my gardens.
SERVANT 1	Certainly sir. Which of your shoes shall I prepare?
KING	Shoes . . . shoes! I'm not walking round the garden! Have my carriage ready at once.
SERVANT 1	Sir.
KING	Servant!
SERVANT 2	Your majesty.
KING	Get my bed ready. After lunch and my ride round the garden, I'm going for a lie down.
SERVANT 2	Yes, your majesty.
READER	Now you can see from this that although the king was young and handsome, he was both lazy and greedy. Two years went by with him living like this.

SCENE 2 Two years later

SVENSON	You called, your majesty.
KING	Yes, my old friend. You know it's been so long since I looked in that great mirror in the state room. Have it brought here.
SVENSON	Of course, your majesty.

The mirror arrives and the king looks in it

Good Morning Everybody Book 2 © Redvers Brandling, Nelson Thornes Ltd, 2002

KING	There's something wrong here! That mirror's not working properly. I've looked in it and it's not me looking back. What I see is a fat, untidy man with puffy cheeks and a pale face. That's not me. Bring me another mirror!
SVENSON	Of course, sir.

Several mirrors are brought in. The king looks in all of them

KING	There's something terribly wrong. They all show the same thing
SVENSON	Absolutely, sir. There's something wrong with them all. The only mirror you can rely on is the mirror of truth. You only get a true picture of yourself in the mirror of truth.
KING	Well bring it here at once then.
SVENSON	I'm sorry, sir, but it's not as easy as that. The mirror of truth is magic and will only work for the person who brings it himself.
KING	Right, get my carriage ready. We'll go and get it.
SVENSON	*coughs discreetly* I'm afraid it can only be found by someone who looks for it on foot, sir.
KING	On foot! On foot! You mean . . . walk!
SVENSON	And there's more, sir.
KING	Well?
SVENSON	It can only be found just after dawn.
KING	But . . . I'm never awake then. Oh well, it must be done I suppose.
SVENSON	I'm afraid there's even more to it, sir.
KING	Go on, go on, tell me.
SVENSON	Well sir, I'm afraid before you go to look for the magic mirror you have to do magic exercises.
KING	I hope this is going to be successful, Svenson – for your sake!

SCENE 3 In the woods

READER	And so King Osric started to get up at dawn. As soon as he was awake he did half an hour's

exercise. Then, after a light breakfast, he went out for long, long walks searching for the mirror of truth. Svenson always went with him. But no matter how hard they looked they could not find the mirror. This went on for six months and then one morning . . .

KING   Come on Svenson, keep up man. If we're walking, let's do it properly.

SVENSON   Yes, sir.

KING   I've got a feeling we're going to find it this morning.

SVENSON   I think you're right sir. In fact that clump of grass over there seems just the sort of place it might be.

KING   Come on then, let's get over there. Wait a minute! I think . . . yes . . . there's something glittering in that grass. It's . . .

SVENSON   Yes! It's the mirror of truth!

KING   Wonderful! After all this time. Now . . .

King picks up mirror and looks into it

KING   Marvellous, Svenson. It is the mirror of truth. Look, it's me again – fit, handsome, upright. At last a mirror that tells the truth!

SVENSON   *a loud cough*

KING   What's the matter?

SVENSON   There's something I need to tell you, your majesty.

KING   Come on then, out with it.

SVENSON   There's no such thing as a magic mirror of truth, sir. That's just an ordinary mirror from the palace.

KING   You mean . . .

SVENSON   Yes, sir. It's not the mirror that's changed, it's you, sir. Now you're back to your old fit self. I hope you'll forgive me, sir.

KING   *long pause* Forgive you! Thank you, Svenson, for making me see sense. You know . . . I like all this exercise. So, even though we've found the mirror I'll still see you for a walk every morning!

Good Morning Everybody Book 2 © Redvers Brandling, Nelson Thornes Ltd, 2002

86 MODESTY

SCENE 1 A cottage in the woods and its garden

MOTHER   Oh my bones are aching.

JOCASTA   Never mind, Mother. I'll do all I can to help.

MOTHER   If only we weren't so poor then you wouldn't have to work so hard. Oh look, that bird is picking seeds from our drying tray in the garden.

JOCASTA   I'll chase it away.

Jocasta goes into the garden

JOCASTA   Shoo bird! I'm sorry but we can't afford to let you have any of our seeds. I'm afraid we're just too poor.

MAGIC BIRD Ah my dear, I've already eaten some. But I'll pay you for what I've eaten.
Come to the tallest tree in the wood at sunset tonight.

SCENE 2 At the tallest tree in the wood

JOCASTA   Bird, bird, are you here?

MAGIC BIRD I'm right here.

Bird appears with a big box

JOCASTA   I'm sorry to bother you but you did say to come.

MAGIC BIRD Of course and I want you to eat with me. Now do you want to eat from a gold dish, a silver dish or a brass dish?

JOCASTA   How kind of you. Just a brass dish please.

Dishes and food are produced from the big box. Girl and bird eat

JOCASTA   That was delicious. Thank you so much.

MAGIC BIRD I enjoyed your company. But I know you must get back to your poor old mother. Now, payment for what I ate. Would you like a gold box, a silver box or a brass box?

JOCASTA You ate so little seed that a brass box will be more than enough.

BIRD Here you are then.

JOCASTA Thank you, you are very kind.

SCENE 3 Back at the cottage

Jocasta and her mother are there. Gretchen is visiting them

MOTHER Shall we open that box now that you're back, Jocasta?

JOCASTA Of course, Mother.

MOTHER It's probably just an empty box . . . but . . .

JOCASTA Oh mother, this beautiful jewel is in the box. It must be worth more money than we have ever had in our lives. How wonderful and how kind of that bird!

GRETCHEN You lucky, lucky people. But how did you come to get a box from a bird?

MOTHER It ate some of our seeds and then said it would pay for what it ate.

GRETCHEN Hmm.

SCENE 4 Gretchen's cottage

The same situation is repeated in Gretchen's cottage. She is there, with a tray of seeds in her garden. The bird arrives and eats some. Gretchen accosts it

GRETCHEN Hey bird, what do you mean by eating our seeds? How dare you! We've hardly got enough for ourselves.

MAGIC BIRD I'm very sorry to hear that but I'll certainly pay for what I've eaten. Come to my home in the tallest tree at sunset.

GRETCHEN I'll certainly be there. You owe us!

SCENE 5 Back at the tallest tree in the wood

GRETCHEN   Hey bird. I'm here.
BIRD   So you are. Well we'd better eat before we do business. Do you want to eat off a gold, silver or brass plate.
GRETCHEN   What do you think? A gold dish of course!
BIRD   Very well.

Dishes, food, etc. come from the large box. The two eat

BIRD   I hope you enjoyed your meal. Now, I must pay you for the seed I ate. Would you like payment in a gold, silver or brass box?
GRETCHEN   I want a gold box.
BIRD   Here you are then. Now off you go back to your mother.

SCENE 6 Back at Gretchen's cottage

GRETCHEN   Look at this, Mother, just look at this. It's our payment in a gold box. If that silly Jocasta got a rich jewel from a grubby brass box think what we'll get from a gold one!
MOTHER   You've done well there girl. Come on – open up.

Gretchen opens box

GRETCHEN   It's a . . . it's a . . . aahhh! It's a snake! Help!

Resources

FOLK TALES

Folk tales are an endless source of good assembly material. Libraries, book shops and publisher's catalogues promote new and up-to-date collections but, by browsing at car boot sales and in charity and second-hand book-shops, you can often unearth some good out-of-date versions.

Some good collections include:

- Robert Ingpen and Barbara Hayes (illus.), *Folk Tales and Fables of Europe* (Dragon's World, 1992) which contains seventeen tales, some very well known, some less so;
- Anne Gatti, *Tales from the African Plains* (Pavilion Books, 1997) which has twelve beautifully illustrated stories with good assembly potential;
- Katie Roden, ed., *Tales from Around the World* (Wayland) is a series of books which embrace stories from Africa, the Caribbean, Central and South America, Egypt, Greece, India, North America, British Isles and Norse and Roman tales;
- Mary Hoffman and Jane Ray (illus.), *Sun, Moon and Stars* (Orion, 1999) is an outstanding blend of beautiful illustrations and unusual stories about the stars in the night sky, some of which are good for drama in assembly;
- Geraldine McCaughrean, *The Orchard Myths* (Orchard Books, 1999 – 2000) is a series of collections of short easy-to-read books.

RELIGIOUS MATERIAL

Teachers will have their own ideas of which are the best biblical sources but for simple retelling of Christian stories there is still no better book than Alan T. Dale, *New World – the best of the New Testament in Plain English* (Oxford University Press). With regard to further biblical material then Redvers Brandling and Robert H. Horton, *A New Introduction to the Bible Books 1–4* (Hodder and Stoughton Educational, 1990) offers a wide range of material, much of which is suitable for direct reading in assembly. In this series there are four books: Stories of God's People; Stories of Jesus and His Teaching; Stories of the Prophets; and Stories of the Early Church. Local sources such as vicars and curates can often provide useful material and alternative presenters!

For comprehesive material on all religions then the School Curriculum and Assessment Authority documents should always be considered as a high priority. Their 'Glossary of Terms' document which covers Christianity, Buddhism, Hinduism, Islam, Judaism and Sikhism is extremely valuable and should be a permanent addition to any primary school's RE resources. With religions other than Christianity, local sources are most important.

CONTEMPORARY MATERIAL

Newspapers are a valuable source of stories about courage, fortitude, hardship, inspiration, injustice, etc. This applies very much to local as well as national publications and a file of cuttings should figure largely in any assembly presenter's collection. The same applies to many magazines. It is also worth having a pen and paper ready to note stories which appear in radio and TV news programmes. Inspiring stories suitable for assemblies can occasionally stem from local sources too such as the police, the fire brigade, nurses, animal wardens, parents and grandparents.

AUDIO-VISUAL MATERIAL

Most schools have a collection of records, tapes, CDs and music books and these often reflect the personal and collective tastes of the staff. The recommendations which follow here are based on the following criteria: that they have all been used with primary children; where there is a requirement for a pianist to play, this could be done by any reasonably competent pianist; and the recorded material is either designed to establish a mood in assembly or is of quality recordings of children and invites sing-along participation.

MUSIC BOOKS

Each assembly in this book contains a hymn suggestion. These are taken from *The Complete Come and Praise* (BBC Educational Publishing, 1990). For those teachers who feel they would like the material for three- to seven-year-olds then there is a *Come and Praise Beginning Collection*. Tapes and CDs are available to support both of these BBC titles.

The Music Sales Group, (see p 195 for contact details) markets music from publishers such as Chester Music, Golden Apple Productions, Novello, Shawnee Press, Youngsong Musicals and World Wide Music. A rich harvest of interesting material can be obtained from this source.

RECORDED MUSIC

All of us respond to the moods which are established through evocative music. For a wide variety of such music, the following examples are suggested. *Scheherazade* offers superb preparatory music for storytelling and the works of Lloyd Webber, Prokofiev, Wagner and Mussorgsky are good for dramatic impact. Spirituals and gospel music are rhythmic and often thought-provoking. Travel music is always useful and themes from films such as *Fiddler on the Roof*, *633 Squadron* and *The Big Country* set an expansive tone. Marches by military bands offer rousing openings and space themes conjure up awesome or mystical feelings. Finally, tapes or CDs of sound effects are very useful.

VISUAL MATERIAL

Posters, pictures, artefacts, displays and collections of children's work are all valuable here. An overhead projector is a valuable support, particularly where commentary requires illustration.

Finally, the occasional use of something familiar can be of value. When this is done, it can help focus on a specific aspects; for instance, *The Lion King* (Dir. Roger Allers: USA, 1994) covers parent/child relationships and the value of friends.

USEFUL ADDRESSES

The following list contains the contact details for the organisations and charities which are mentioned in 'Information for the teacher'. For further information about their work and the topics covered in the assemblies, use the addresses provided below.

Barnardo's
Address: Tanners Lane, Ilford, Essex, IG6 1QG
Website: www.barnardos.org.uk

Battersea Dogs' Home
Address: 4 Battersea Park Road, London SW8 4AA
Website: www.dogshome.org

British Red Cross
Address: 9 Grosvenor Crescent, London, SW1X 7EJ
Website: www.redcross.org.uk

British Parachute Association
Address: Wharf Way, Glen Parva, Leicester, LE2 9TF
Website: www.bpa.org.uk

Children of Courage Awards
Address: Woman's Own, Stamford Street, London SE1 9LF

Christian Aid
Address: 35 Lower Marsh, Waterloo, London, SE1 7RT
Website: www.christian-aid.org.uk

Christian Education Movement
Address: Royal Buildings, Victoria Street, Derby, DE1 1GW
Website: www.cem.org.uk

Guide Dogs for the Blind Association
Address: Burghfield Common, Reading, RG7 3YG
Website: www.gdba.org.uk

Hearing Dogs for the Deaf
Address: London Road, Lewknor, Oxon, OX49 5RY
Website: www.hearing-dogs.co.uk

Music Sales Group
Address: Education Department, Newmarket Road, Bury St Edmunds, Suffolk, 1P33 3YB

Redwings Horse Sanctuary
Address: Hapton, Norwich, Norfolk, NR15 1SP
Website: www.redwings.org.uk

Robin Hood information
Address: Robin Hood Collection, Central Library, Angel Row, Nottingham NG1 6HP
Website: www.robinhood.ltd.uk/robinhood/legend.html

Royal Association for Disability and Rehabilitation (RADAR)
Address: 12 City Forum, 250 City Road, London, EC1V 8AF
Website: www.radar.org.uk

Royal Life Saving Society (RLSS)
Address: River House, High Street, Broom, Warwickshire, B50 4HN
Website: www.lifesavers.org.uk

Royal National Lifeboat Institution (RNLI)
Address: West Quay Road, Poole, Dorset B15 1HZ
Website: www.rnli.org.uk

Royal National Mission to Deep Sea Fishermen
Address: 43 Nottingham Place, London W1M 4BX
Website: www.fishing-news.co.uk/rnmdsf

Royal Society for the Prevention of Accidents (RoSPA)
Address: Edgbaston Park, 353 Bristol Road, Edgbaston, Birmingham B5 7ST
Website: www.rospa.co.uk

Royal Society for the Prevention of Cruelty to Animals (RSPCA)
Address: Wilberforce Way, Southwater, Horsham, West Sussex, RH13 7WN
Website: www.rspca.org.uk

Samaritans
Address: 10 The Grove, Slough, Berkshire, SL1 1QP
Website: www.samaritans.org.uk

SHAP Working Party (calendar of religious festivals)
Address: c/o The National Society's RE Centre, 36 Causton Street, London, SW1P 4AU
Website: www.support4learning.org.uk